W0017104

Cultural Critique

94 The State of Things

Fall
2016

Book Reviews

EDITORIAL STATEMENT

Cultural Critique provides a forum for creative and provocative scholarship in the theoretical humanities and humanistic social sciences. Transnational in scope and transdisciplinary in orientation, the journal strives to spark and galvanize intellectual debates as well as to attract and foster critical investigations regarding any aspect of culture as it expresses itself in words, images, and sounds, across both time and space. The journal is especially keen to support scholarship that engages the ways in which cultural production, cultural practices, and cultural forms constitute and manifest the nexus between the aesthetic, the psychic, the economic, the political, and the ethical intended in their widest senses. While informed by the diverse traditions of historical materialism as well as by the numerous critiques of such traditions from various parts of the globe, the journal welcomes contributions based on a variety of theoretical–methodological paradigms.

Cultural Critique appears three times a year. General issues, including essays, book reviews, and thematic sections, as well as entire issues devoted to special topics, are regularly published. The editors welcome the submission of freestanding essays, special issue proposals on topics of interest to the journal, as well as reviews of relevant, new, and not-so-new books.

Cultural Critique Books is the companion series of the journal. It seeks to attract work by those scholars across the humanities and social sciences who continue to draw inspiration from, and seek to contribute to, the theoretical movements and debates so long nurtured at Minnesota. Book proposals should be addressed to one of the three editors at: *Cultural Critique*, Department of Cultural Studies and Comparative Literature, 235 Nicholson Hall, 216 Pillsbury Drive S.E., University of Minnesota, Minneapolis, MN 55455-0229, U.S.A., or via email to cultcrit@umn.edu.

RESTATING THINGS, AGAIN

John Mowitt and Cesare Casarino

Jochen Schulte-Sasse, in memoriam

Difference and repetition: such is, at best, the celebration of an anniversary, of a recurrence. This special issue of *Cultural Critique* marks a recurrence and aspires to repetition with difference: it collects the papers delivered at the symposium on "The State of Things" that took place at the University of Minnesota in October 2015 to celebrate the thirtieth anniversary of the foundation of the journal. We celebrated with a symposium, an event that precisely in restating and restaging the inexhaustible encounter between historical materialism and psychoanalysis effectively predicted our appeal here to the friction within and between difference and repetition.

Recall that Plato's remarkable dialogue "The Symposium" begins with a street scene. Let's be more precise. It is a moment of interpellation. Apollodorus, interrupted in medias res, reports that while out earlier Glaucon had hailed him demanding to know about the dinner that had "recently" occurred at Agathon's during which guests, including Socrates and Aristophanes, discoursed about love. Plato has Glaucon call out: "Hey, I say, Apollodorus, can't you wait for me?" Barely slowing, Apollodorus somewhat breathlessly explains that Glaucon is deluded, having apparently forgotten that the event in question took place years earlier and that what he, Apollodorus, knows about it he has learned second or third hand.

It is common now to point to the self-defeating deployment of myth by Plato as evidence of the tragic entanglement of philosophy and literature, but if we insist on the peculiar opening of the symposium— the spirals of reported speech, the echoing delays—it is because we want to remind ourselves that what has been called "literary technique" operates within and on philosophy in far more tenacious ways. In this spirit one might also wish to point, within "The Symposium" in particular, to the morphological cliché of Diotima—whose Iriga-rayan affirmation of the "between two" effectively crashes what is otherwise a stag party.

But why linger over such details?

When one of us assumed his position at Minnesota in 1985 (hav-ing visited earlier), this was the entanglement in which he found him-self. It was a situation about which he was largely quiet—quiet until the advent of *Cultural Critique,* an academic journal launched by his colleague in English, Donna Przybylowicz, and her partner Abdul Jan-Mohamed. As is typical of such inaugural gestures, it was tied to an international conference convened at the University of Minnesota dur-ing which many provocative papers were read and debated, several of which later appeared in the first issue of the journal. Listening to these, and even more importantly, witnessing new colleagues listen-ing to them, made it less daunting to whisper of such entanglements, to take them seriously as more than personal failings. Or, to suddenly recognize the hidden rigors of personal failings. Whatever. The point is that in tandem with the Theory and History of Literature series at the University of Minnesota Press, *Cultural Critique,* this indestructi-ble orange but black box, was pinging the hope that led several of us to this university, including the other one of us, who had started read-ing the journal in the late 1980s while struggling with similar entan-glements as a graduate student and who eventually made his way westward and landed at the University of Minnesota first and then onto the flight deck of the journal itself.

Another reason for lingering over the textual details of "The Sym-posium" now suggests itself–namely, to invoke Michel Foucault's invo-cation of René Magritte: this was not a conference, and these are not conference proceedings. If *Cultural Critique* was born with a confer-ence, the symposium commemorating this birth thirty years later was an attempt to do something different: to commemorate publicly not exactly love (though love did come up) but the coming together of wisdom lovers to think, in common, about the "state of things." This thinking was a bit more staged than the event at Agathon's—we did task particular individuals with stirring our thought—but the goal remained the same, at once serious yet festive (in all its connotations). When not translated as "The Symposium" this dialogue is also referred to as "The Drinking Party," and this is entirely fair, especially as the evening at Agathon's implacably descends into an ironman competition won, as many will know, by Socrates. Although we too did drink, this was at bottom a potluck, as our feasting was firstly aimed at chewing over the ideas regarding the "state of things" that everyone had brought, as it were, to the table. We invited Jacqueline Rose, Jodi Dean, and David Marriott to come and tell us about the "state of things," and Jane Blocker, Tony C. Brown, and Paula Rabinowitz to respond to their thoughts—and, last yet not least, our coeditor and fellow traveler, Simona Sawhney, responded from Delhi to all, stating the closing words in the form of an apostrophe, its own distinctive form of a different repetition. We listened, we talked, we even fought. We hope now—by offering this feast in print—to stir you in turn.

It seems fitting, under the circumstances, to observe that as concerns academic publications the "state of things" is vexed. The "disintegration of *the* public sphere" worried over by Jürgen Habermas now almost half a century ago has only recently shown its true colors: disintegration through hyperinflation, a term whose economic overtones point directly to the neoliberal logic of assessment and calculation whereby journals are disassembled and redistributed across open access portals, word counts, moving walls, citation indices, and the like. While this may feel like the "end of the book" we have been anticipating since 1967, it is in fact the penumbral lip of the end of the research university, the global ascendency of Anglophone iThought. Under such circumstances, *parrhesia* is far from enough. The sort of rash obstinacy we hope will be fed at this feast is both essential and required. We will let the reader decide where repetition and where difference lie.

John Mowitt and **Cesare Casarino** are, with Simona Sawhney, senior editors of *Cultural Critique*.

FEMINISM AND THE ABOMINATION
OF VIOLENCE

When I was working on Sylvia Plath more than twenty years
ago, I discovered that, almost simultaneously, the distinguished critic
and biographer Diane Middlebrook was working on Anne Sexton.
Upon completion of our books—we shared at least one train ride on
our way to readings across England—we were both in a state of not
only exhilaration but also shock. Both poets had required us—a
requirement each of us experienced as an exclusive, personal, invitation—to immerse ourselves in what it meant to suffer as a woman in
the 1950s and early 1960s. But they did so with such vigor and riotous-
ness as to deprive us of, or at least exceed, the most obvious narrative
of subordination that you might expect such suffering to evoke. Sexton and Plath were angry—they had a lot to be angry about. But in both
cases, the anger did not block, as it so easily can, the complex internal
reckoning that as women they conducted with themselves.[1]

If this central reality united our projects and fueled our respect and
love for the two poets, it also overrode what was the most striking dis-
crepancy between our experiences in writing our books. At every turn,
I (like so many Plath scholars) had been obstructed by the Plath estate,
Olwyn and then Ted Hughes, who hated my book, and insisted it was
a biography, which it wasn't.[2] They felt I had transgressed the boundary
between literary criticism and life story, a life story whose true version
they knew themselves, without reserve, to be in sole possession of.
Diane's problem was the opposite. If anything the Sexton estate had
been too cooperative, flooding her with what today we call "too much
information," whether in the form of the release by Sexton's analyst of
the tapes she made after her sessions at his instruction to prevent her
obliterating them from her mind or in the revelations by Sexton's
daughter, pressed on Diane, of being intimately invaded by her mother.

If that moment has stayed with me, it is because of the ethical dilemma we both faced. Neither Sexton nor Plath lived to see the birth of second-wave feminism. It is tempting, and not wholly inappropriate, to think that if they had enjoyed the advantage of feminist insight and solidarity they might both have been alive today. Certainly, their anguish as women was rooted in the perils of domesticity and child-rearing, which would become the target of that wave of feminism's opening and loudest complaint and for which they were among the first to craft the poetic language, to give it voice. But that was not all. Sexton was an emotional hurricane. At the center of that hurricane there is a tale of domestic abuse—by her father, possibly by her beloved aunt, later of her own daughter. As this story migrates across genders and generations, there is no neat version to be told. It swallows up too many people, regurgitates through Sexton's life and writing (such regurgitation is of course recognized today as the hallmark of abuse). Plath, for her part, felt herself trapped by a desire that drowned her in its intensity and left her stranded on the far shore of a domestic ideal that was a travesty of her own fierce and expansive imaginative reach.

What we shared was our respect for the psychic risks that being a poet allowed both these women to take, together with the conviction that the energy with which they did so is more important than the fact of their deaths. "What I most want to know about women in the past" is not, therefore, as Catherine MacKinnon puts it in an article first published in 1992, "how did she die?" but rather, "how did she live?" (2006a, 28). And I also want that question to be able to gather on its journey whatever it may find, however messy and unexpected, on its path. Central to what follows is the proposition that feminism has nothing to gain by seeing women solely or predominantly as the victims of their histories.

If I quote MacKinnon it is not just because she represents a viewpoint from which I dissent nor because I know there are many feminist scholars who draw productively from her work. It is also because, as she has most loudly and consistently alerted us, the times we live in oblige any feminist to reckon with the increasing, or certainly increasingly visible, violence against women that we seem to be witnessing today. In March 2014, Gayatri Spivak gave the Juliet Mitchell Lecture in Cambridge on rape as both a—if not *the*—crime of identity and as the "indestructible unconditionality" of the human: "We are," she stated, "male and female—raped into humanity." "This is," she stated, "the human condition."[3] This did not, of course, stop her from naming rape as the crime against women which it mostly is. Feminism today cannot *not* talk about such crimes, whether rape as a war crime, fgm, or domestic abuse. To pluck just one out of a barrage of recent statistics and reports, a survey of forty-two thousand women across twenty-eight EU member states released in March 2014 found violence against women to be an extensive human rights abuse throughout Europe, with one in three women reporting some form of physical or sexual abuse since the age of fifteen and the UK reporting the joint fifth highest incidence of physical and sexual violence.[4] Most of that violence is carried out by a current or former partner with nearly one in four women in relationships reporting partner abuse. Disturbingly, the incidence of abuse does not seem to decline with a rise in equality. Violence against women in Denmark, Finland, and Sweden, each praised for their gender equality, outstrips the UK rate. Central to the problem is that domestic abuse is one of the least-reported crimes.[5] The statistics are therefore, as always, misleading, in the case of such abuse perhaps even more so than usual. In discussion of these reports, we hear little of the obstacles that litter the path between sexual violation, indeed between all sexuality, and language (where it is not just a matter of finding the courage to speak)—compounded of course by the institutionalized refusal of those in positions of authority to listen.

Domestic abuse is not the worst, but I do not want to list all the forms of global violence against women as it is one feminist tactic to do. Feminism is not served by turning violence into a litany, as if the only way to make us think about such violence is by verbally driving it home, rubbing it in our face, as one might say. When we look at the picture of a woman who died on 9/11, the first and only feminist question should not, to my mind, be—MacKinnon again—"who hurt her before?" (2006a, 28); nor, when we look at the bones of a woman from an ancient civilization, do I want us to see her, and them, as, inevitably, broken. Such a strategy does not help us to think. It is a central argument of this essay that violence against women is a crime of the deepest thoughtlessness. It is a sign that the mind has brutally blocked itself. The best way, I argue, for feminism to counter violence against women is to speak of, to stay and reckon with, the extraordinary, often painful, and mostly overlooked, range of what the human mind is capable of.

The title of this essay is "Feminism and the Abomination of Violence." Violence for me is part of the psyche. A crime to be detested and cast off but also something that one feminism, in the very force of that gesture—however necessary, however right at one level—then itself repudiates, renders unthinkable, shuns beyond the remit of the human (precisely abominates). At that moment, feminism finds itself replicating that part of the mind that cannot tolerate its own complexity. It thereby becomes complicit with the psychic processes that lead to the enactment of violence itself. For me it then becomes crushing—or to put it more crassly, cuts off its nose to spite its face.

I take my idea of thoughtlessness from Hannah Arendt, to whom—along with Melanie Klein—I appeal here as offering a new way of thinking about violence against women in our time. Following and anticipating Sexton and Plath, both Arendt and Klein suggest that there is something about the process of human thought that is often insufferable, not least because thinking acts as a break on the fantasy that the world is there to be mastered and thereby prevents that dangerous fantasy from doing untold damage by running amuck or away with itself. For Arendt, violence is a form of radical self-deceit—or "the impotence of bigness," to use her phrase—that punishes the world, punishes women we can say, for the limitations of human power (the gender implications of her phrase "impotence of bigness" are surely glaring even if she does not fully draw them out herself) (1972, 34). "What I propose, therefore, is very simple," she writes at the beginning of *The Human Condition*, "it is nothing more than to think about what we are doing" (1958, 5). As often with Arendt, such simplicity is deceptive. Thinking as process has to be fought for. It is threatened from all sides, by modern pseudoknowledge which leaves us at the mercy of every gadget that is technically possible "however murderous it is," and by the muteness of sheer violence: "Only sheer violence," she writes, "is mute" (6). For Arendt, therefore, the mind is under siege, and thinking is the only restraint against murderous know-how and the cruel silence of sheer violence which mutes both itself and its victims.

Arendt wrote *The Human Condition* in the 1950s (it was published in 1958)—the moment, of course, of Sexton and Plath—when the power of death-dealing technology had reached new heights: from industrial genocide to the atom bomb. "The technical development of the implements of violence," she writes in her later 1970 study *On Violence*, "has now reached a point where no political goal could conceivably correspond to their destructive potential or justify their actual use in armed conflict" (1970a, 3). The "suicidal" development of modern weapons involves "a massive intrusion of criminal violence into politics" (14). Behind this analysis is her indictment of the myth of "progress" which the United States, where she arrived as a refugee from Nazism in the 1930s, believed itself to embody beyond any other nation (today's version would be Hillary Clinton describing the United States as the "indispensable nation," which of course sanctions any worldwide intervention the United States wishes to make). For Arendt, "progress" is a ruthless illusion, a self-fulfilling prophecy, which leaves itself no escape clause other than the increasingly violent enactment of itself. Or to put it another way, so-called progress leads directly to the burnt bodies of Vietnam.

Arendt is not, to put it mildly, most famous for her contribution to feminism, any more indeed than Melanie Klein, on which more later, although the case for Arendt's contribution to feminism has been made strongly by scholars such as Seyla Benhabib and Mary Dietz, whose readings are the starting points for mine.[6] But there is an important gender dimension to her work (and, as I argue, to Klein's). It is there in that "impotent bigness"—a phrase to which I will return. But, almost despite herself, Arendt can be seen as the forerunner of one feminist analysis that traces women's subordination, and the violence that is so often its consequence, first and foremost to the division of labor in—or rather consignment of women *to*—the home. Arendt's political ideal is the Greek city space of the polis. Indeed, so invested is she in the Athenian model of democracy that she has often been accused of overlooking (or worse, reinforcing) the status of women and slaves on whose bodies and backs it built itself. But Arendt makes it clear that if the home and family life are prepolitical, it is because, she writes, they are the place "where the household head ruled with uncontested despotic powers" (1958, 27). It is because the paterfamilias rules with such absolute power in the household that it remains outside the domain of politics: "Even the power of the tyrant was less great, less 'perfect' than the power with which the *paterfamilias,* the *dominus,* ruled over the household of slaves and family" (27).

The consequence is violence in the home. Freedom belonged exclusively in the political realm, whereas the household was the place of necessity—read the base environment of creaturely life (or "house-work," as we call it today)—that must be mastered for man to be free. Out of this forced discrimination, violence surely follows. Because, in Greek thought, "all human beings are subject to necessity," Arendt explains, "they are entitled to violence towards others" (1958, 31). Violence then becomes the "pre-political act of liberating oneself from the necessity of life for the freedom of the world" (31). That is why to be a slave means, not just loss of freedom, but being subject to man-made violence. And this is also why there is no real sexual division of labor—nothing one could even grace with the epithet of "separate spheres"—since such a notion relies on an at least formal assumption of equality between man and women, whereas no such assumption existed. Women and slaves—Arendt is surely hardly condoning the equation—stand in, and for, the place where the necessity of the world is subject to brute mastery. While the ancient household head might of course exert a milder or harsher rule, he knows "neither law nor justice" (34). Or to put it another way, it is because women and slaves are called on to redeem the frailty of human, bodily, life—what Judith Butler would call "precarious life"—that they are the objects, in fact they *must be* the objects, of violence.

The key word is "mastery." It is for Arendt, in the world and in the heart, a delusion. Thus when she goes on to make her famous distinction between violence and power that is at the center of *On Violence,* what matters is that a government will have recourse to violence in direct proportion to a decline in its authority and power, a decline that violence is desperate to redress (violence is always desperate). "Rule by sheer violence," she writes, "comes about when power is being lost" (1970a, 53). State violence, we could say, is the last resort of the criminal (as we have seen so cruelly in the crackdown on the streets of Egypt, post–Tahrir Square, and throughout the world). When a state "starts to devour its own children," Arendt observes, "power has disappeared completely" (think Syria) (55). "We know or should know," she insists, "that every decrease in power is an open invitation to violence—if only because those who hold power and feel it slipping from their hands . . . have always found it difficult to resist the temptation to substitute violence for it" (87). And she observes: "Impotence breeds violence and psychologically this is quite true" (54).

Arendt's distinction between violence and power is important in relation to a feminism that wishes to align violence with male power of which it then becomes the inevitable expression (which makes female power, as MacKinnon once famously put it, "a contradiction in terms" [1988, 53]). Instead, Arendt allows us to see such an equation as the lie that violence *perpetuates about itself,* since it will do anything—destroy women and the world—rather than admit that its power is uncertain. Women then become the scapegoats for man's unconscious knowledge of his own human, which means shared—that is, *shared with women*— frailty ("The Frailty of Human Affairs" is the title of one section of *The Human Condition*). Such frailty takes us to the darkest corridors of life and of the mind, to "the realm of birth and death" that must be excluded from the public realm because "it harbors the things hidden from human eyes and impenetrable to human knowledge. Impenetrable because man does not know where he comes from when he is born and where he goes where he dies" (1958, 62–63). Or to put it another way, violence is man's response to the fraudulence of his power and the limits of his knowledge. "Impotent bigness" indeed, as we might say.

In her constant return to what cannot be mastered or fully known by the mind, Arendt, as I read her, is—perilously or brilliantly depending on your viewpoint—skirting the domain of psychoanalysis for which her stated antipathy is well known. But it is very hard not to read her account of things impenetrable to the human mind as having much in common with the Freudian concept of the unconscious that signals—over and above the sexual debris of its contents—the limits of man's cognizance of the world and of himself. In Arendt's account such limits strike the body politic as much as they do the human heart. This is her vocabulary for both these realms: "boundlessness," "unpredictability," and "the darkness of the human heart" (1958, 244, 191). We live, she states, in an "ocean of uncertainty," against which there is no redress (1958, 244). It is the human condition. Men are fundamentally unreliable since they "can never guarantee who they will be tomorrow" (244). And how, she asks, can you see or foretell the consequences of an act "within a community of equals where everybody has the same capacity to act" (244)? To be part of the body politic means relinquishing your control over the future—yours and that of the other who is your equal, *because* they are your equal. Man's "inability to rely upon himself or have complete faith in himself," which, she

insists, "is the same thing," is "the price human beings pay for freedom" (244). While "the impossibility of remaining unique master of
what they do"—read subordinating another to your power—"is the
price they pay for plurality and reality" (244). If Arendt describes such
open, equal, participation in the unpredictable reality of the world
as a "joy" (her word), she has also laid out with stunning clarity the
unwelcome nature of her own insight and, hence, the lengths men will
go to deny that insight and subordinate the world, in which I include
women, to his purpose.

In *The Life of the Mind*, which was Arendt's last work, she takes
this further. Now thinking appears even more clearly as the other side
of false mastery and knowledge. This is why, for example, Arendt insists
that the correct translation of Kant's *Verstand* is not "understanding"
but "intellect" or "cognition," because it represents the "desire to know,"
as distinct from *Vernunft*, which arises from the "urgent need to think"
(1978, 1:57). "To expect truth to come from thinking," she writes, "signifies that we mistake the need to think with the urge to know," a need
"that can never be assuaged" (1:61, 1:55). Both are anguished but one
in the service of hammering the world into place, the other by its own
interminable process, which has no end on which it can brand its
name. Only intellect or cognition believes it can answer the unanswer-
able questions—that it can seize the world in its mental coil. Philosophers of this persuasion, she tells us, are "like children trying to catch
smoke by closing their hands" (1:122).

Against this false and futile knowing, Arendt places, even more
strikingly in this last meditation, a thinking ego that moves among
"invisible" essences, that is strictly speaking "nowhere," "homeless in
an emphatic sense," which led, she suggests, to the early rise of "cos-
mopolitanism" amongst philosophers (1978, 1:199). Way ahead of her
time, Arendt calls up her answer to the violence of the times in the
terms—homeless, nowhere, cosmopolitan—that will be so central to
the literary and cultural theory that will follow, although rarely acknowledge, her. And in doing so, she shows these terms seized from the history of the refugee and the exile—homeless, nowhere—the stateless,
as we might say, whose predicament had been her own and which she
did so much to articulate and dignify. True thought, then, is a form of
memory that exerts no dominion, ousts no one from their own space,
because it remembers that it is or once was radically homeless. We

could not be further from the despotic ruler of the Athenian household who dispenses violence to his women and slaves because it is in
the remit of his own power, or rather because it is the only way he can
struggle to exert control over the debasing, corporal, necessities of life.
Nor from the modern-day state that turns to violence in order to shore
up a power that has lost all legitimacy. Arendt's life of the mind does
not, then, point to some realm of abstract contemplation—her plea for
thought is the child of its time.

Perhaps then we should not be surprised, although I admit that I
was, to find Arendt slowly inching her way to the world of the dream—
the "royal road to the unconscious," as Freud called it (till the end of
his life, he saw *The Interpretation of Dreams* as his most important book).
Whatever the achievements of the thinking ego, it will, Arendt writes,
never be able to "convince itself that anything actually exists and that
life, human life, is more than a dream" (1978, 1:198). To illustrate this
suspicion—among the most characteristic of Asian philosophy—she
then selects the Taoist story of Chuang Tzu who dreamt he was a butterfly only to wake not to the unerring sureness of who he really was
but to the realization that perhaps he was a butterfly dreaming he was
Chuang Tzu (the same example used by Jacques Lacan to evoke the
vanishing of the human subject in relation to the unconscious [Arendt
1978, 1:198; Lacan 2004, 76]). But Arendt (being Arendt) does not of
course leave it there. The dream returns—in the conclusion to *The Life
of the Mind*—as the great equalizer in the shape of the king who dreams
he is an artisan (since his quotient of life in that moment is no different
from the poor artisan who dreams he is king) (Arendt 1978, 2:150).
Moreover, she writes, since "'one frequently dreams that he is dreaming'" (she is citing Pascal's critique of Descartes), "nothing can guarantee that what we call our life is not wholly a dream from which we
shall awaken in death" (2:150). The personal resonance of such moments
in this, her last, uncompleted, book, is surely striking. Arendt is exploring and relinquishing her own powers.

Something is creeping back into Arendt's writing. Remember the
Greek citizen who mingled freely in the polis on condition of ruling
with a rod of iron in his home. Remember too that, if women had to
be subdued, it was because women were required to subdue in turn,
and on his behalf, the messy, bodily frailties of life, the realm of birth
and death that "harbors the things hidden from human eyes and

impenetrable to human knowledge." What seems, therefore, to be happening here is that this banished domain of the Greco-Roman dispensation is, in this final work, taking vengeance on the murderous technocratic know-how of the modern world, as slowly but surely it beats a path back into modernity as its only hope. I think we are talking about the return of the repressed. The options are stark. Violence or the dark, shadowy, innermost recesses of the hearth and heart where all knowing comes to grief. Violence or the world of the dream.

Cue Melanie Klein. But before leaving Arendt for Klein, there is a crucial link to be made to Rosa Luxemburg, for whom Arendt's enthusiasm knew no limits. There is the deepest and fully acknowledged debt. In all the works by Arendt I have been discussing so far, spontaneity—Luxemburg's central concept and another humble reminder of the unpredictable reality of the world—is a repeated refrain.[7] But there is one moment when Arendt evokes Luxemburg that is of particular value for what I am trying to evoke here. She is talking about love. In its highest manifestation, Arendt writes, the willing ego pronounces, "*Amo: Volo ut sis*," meaning "I love you; I want you to be." Not, she goes on, "I want to have you," or "I want to rule you" (1978, 2:136). Love without tyranny. Compare this free-wheeling, uncontrolling version of love with Rosa Luxemburg. "Blessed are those without passion," she wrote to her last lover, Hans Diefenbach—a relationship conducted by correspondence from prison—"if that means they would never claw like a panther at the happiness and freedom of others." Then she qualifies: "That has nothing to do with passion. . . . I possess enough of it to set a prairie on fire, and still hold sacred the freedom and the simple wishes of other people" (qtd. in Ettinger 1986, 213). True passion stakes no claim. Like democracy, it does not own, control, or master the other. It lets the other be. With Luxemburg, you barely have to scratch the surface. We are talking about sexual politics.

In the middle of World War II, the pioneering psychoanalyst Melanie Klein finds herself with an unexpected opportunity—to analyze a ten-year-old boy over what they both know in advance will be the restricted time frame of four months. She takes notes after every session—several verbatim—and then collects them into one of the first full-length accounts of what her editor Elliott Jacques describes in his foreword to the published volume as a "total analysis" (5). The fact that this is only made possible by the conditions of the war—evacuation from London—a war which will color the analysis at every turn, is seen not as an obstacle but as the core of the process. Richard's distress is multilayered and overdetermined. This in itself demonstrates the futility of trying to locate childhood anxiety either inside the mind or outside in the world (as if one precluded the other). He is an avid follower of the war—reads three newspapers a day, listens to all the news on the wireless, and threatens suicide at the fall of Crete if Britain should be defeated. But his fear of Hitler is overlaid—driven, perhaps, we do not have to decide—certainly matched, by his fear of his father. The two are inseparable. And what he fears most from his father is what he is doing, or capable of doing, to his mother.

"Just now he had spoken of the terrible things the Austrian Hitler did to the Austrians. By this he meant that Hitler was in a way ill-treating his own people, including Mrs K., just as the bad Daddy would ill-treat Mummy" (Klein, 22). Or again: "Mrs K. interpreted R's desire for peace and order in the family, his giving way to Daddy's and Paul's authority, as a means of restraining his jealousy and hatred. This meant there would be no Hitler-Daddy, and Mummy would not be turned into the 'pig-sty' Mummy, for she would not be injured and bombed by the bad father" (194). Hitler-Daddy. Klein's interpretations are famously blunt, some would say coercive. But this very bluntness, I would like to suggest, has served to obscure something that is also staring us in the face. "Ill-treat," "injure," "bomb"; Mummy as a "pig-sty" for the garbage of the world and of the heart. Like Arendt, Klein is not best renowned as a feminist thinker. Nonetheless, when she looks into Richard's fantasy world, what she sees there—what she urges him to see—is a scene of domestic violence. At one point Richard asks obsessively and solicitously about the number of Klein's other, especially child, patients. Interpreting this as the rivalry and fear of displacement it clearly is, she then also suggests that perhaps he wishes Mrs. Klein to have child patients in the same way as he wanted Mummy to have babies: because *they were less dangerous than men* (347, emphasis added).

It is central to one radical feminist argument that the world of war and peace are no different. For MacKinnon, the 1990s assault on Bosnian women and their resistance to it challenges "the lines between genocide and war and, ultimately, between war and peace" (2006b, 2).

The significance of September 11, which she describes as an "exemplary day of male violence," is that the number of people killed in the twin towers on that day was almost identical to the number of women murdered by men, mostly their male partners, in the United States over the average year (2006c, 260–61). MacKinnon is rightly challenging the indifference of national and international law toward violence against women compared with the military response to the attacks of 9/11. Although when she asks, "Do these women not count as casualties in some war? Will the Marines not land for them?" (2006c, 272), I take my leave. To my mind the last thing feminists should be calling for is the U.S. Marines landing anywhere in the world any more than they do, mostly disastrously, already (although the advent of the drone today means that soldiers do not land at all).

But what is never discussed in this argument, which assumes a perfect fit or continuity between manhood and a violence of which it becomes the supreme and deadly fulfillment, is the terrain in which men, and before them boys, do psychic battle. Crucially, in Klein's account, that terrain is not free of violence. It is drenched in it. She is the arch theorist of psychic violence, more specifically of matricide, as Julia Kristeva points out in her study of Klein.[8] In the case of Richard, the line between war and peace is indeed thin to the point of breaking. To differentiate them is his most urgent task. It is the work to be done. Richard's challenge, we might say, is to resist the pull of the most deadly masculine identifications the world has on offer. Were that not an available option for him, indeed for men more generally, then feminism would surely be on a hiding to nothing, it would be on a losing battle—forever. If the child is father to the man, then, Melanie Klein's life's work suggests, what that means is always, urgently and painfully, up for grabs. There is always still everything to play for.

If there is a profound link here for me to the ideas of Hannah Arendt, it comes through the category of thought. Richard is a boy who "knows his blows" (a slip of the tongue as fateful as it is wondrous) (Klein, 34). Goebbels and Ribbentrop become especially intense objects of hatred when they dare to say that Britain was the aggressor in the war. In this flagrant act of projection, they are way behind Richard himself, since the whole of his analysis is an inner negotiation with the violence that he feels himself capable of. He knows his blows. Remember that lying was the target of some of Arendt's fiercest political critiques ("Lying in Politics," which gave rise to her idea of impotent bigness, was the title of her 1972 critique of the Vietnam War). Lying is, as we know, the collateral damage of warfare whose first casualty is truth. Klein is providing the psychic backdrop to Arendt's protest against the corruption and deceptions of political life, which are if anything more flagrant today. In Richard's narrative, lying is a form of self-harm, an act of blinding that then becomes the trigger for increasing violence against the other. When Klein suggests that Richard's moral outrage at Ribbentrop's lies might be due to the fact that he too is capable of aggression, I read her as saying that the one who deceives himself on such matters becomes his own—although by no means only his own—worst enemy. Lying drives aggression in deeper, leaving it no outlet finally other than the destruction of everything that litters its path (Hitler-Daddy assaulting pig-sty Mummy). When Klein offers this interpretation, Richard remains silent, "obviously thinking over the interpretation and then smiled." When she asks him why he had smiled, "he answered that it was because he liked thinking" (25). This does not mean that he mentally submits to her or lacks his own psychic freedom: "How," he insists at one moment, "can you really know what I think?" (111).

For psychoanalysis, thinking is not of course exactly thinking as it is most commonly understood. Returning to Arendt's insistence on the Kantian difference between the "urge to know" and the "need to think," we could say that psychoanalysis pitches its tent firmly on the side of the latter. Unconscious thinking does not know its own ends. Epistemophilia, as the strongest impulse of the infant, was a term introduced by Klein into the psychoanalytic lexicon. We yearn to know (*Sehnsucht*, or "yearning," was Rosa Luxemburg's favorite word). Driven by sexual curiosity, the infant is pitched into a dark, shadowy world where she or he will struggle to find a place and that she or he cannot fully control, an "ocean of uncertainty," as Arendt might say. Such control would be as murderous as it is phony. It is the violent solution of the bad father who lashes out at the mother as a way of getting rid of what he cannot bear to countenance in himself.

In this sense, Melanie Klein can be seen as the silent psychoanalytic partner of Hannah Arendt. Klein, we might say, is giving flesh and blood to the "passions of the hearth" outlawed from the polis by the Greek city-state. And for Klein, as for Arendt, what is at issue is once again what we might call "impotent bigness." "Richard's love was genuine," she comments, "when his predominant attitude was to protect me against the bad father, or when he himself felt persecuted by the internal father and expected protection from me"—that is, when Richard refuses the invitation to identify with the violent father in his head (426). "He became artificial and insincere," she continues, "*when he felt he possessed the powerful penis with which he could ally himself in a hostile and dangerous way against me*" (426). Only a boy who relinquishes the fantasy of the powerful penis will stop himself from attacking the mother. Ceding his omnipotence at the very moment he is most com-pelled by it is the only path to a viable masculinity—calling the bluff on impotent bigness, as we might say. Certainly it is the only way that this young boy, on the verge of puberty, can behave toward his woman analyst like a gentleman. Or to put it another way, violence against women is the boy's deepest wish and worst fantasy. But if he knows this, can give it thought, then it becomes a fantasy he is less likely to act on.

If Klein is key to this discussion, it is because she is sentient of just how high the stakes are, how treacherous the ground on which she moves. She is dealing with psychotic anxiety in which she believes all human subjects have their share. The greatest anxiety that afflicts the infant is that she or he has destroyed the object; a fear that she distin-guishes crucially from the anxiety that she or he might do so (which at least leaves open the possibility that you and the world might sur-vive). On such finely graded psychic distinctions the health of her patients relies. Hitler-Daddy goes on killing because he has nothing left to lose. For Klein, to skirt this perilous domain in the analytic en-counter is, therefore, a sop to a world in denial (the lies of Ribbentrop). The implications for her practice—what made her and still I think makes her so controversial—resides in this. It was also at the heart of her famous dispute with Anna Freud.[9] In an extended footnote to the twenty-first session with Richard, she explains why she goes so far and why she believes it makes her patients better:

> It is in fact striking that very painful interpretations—and I am particu-larly thinking of the interpretaptions referring to death and to dead inter-nalised objects, which is a psychotic anxiety—could have the effect of

reviving hope and making the patient feel more alive. My explanation for this would be that bringing a very deep anxiety nearer to consciousness, in itself produces relief. But I also believe that the very fact that the analysis gets into contact with deep-lying unconscious anxieties gives the patient a feeling of being understood and therefore revives hope. I have often met in adult patients the strong desire to have been analysed as a child. This was not only because of the obvious advantages of child analysis, but in retrospect the deep longing for having one's unconscious understood had come to the fore. Very understanding and sympathetic parents—and that can also apply to other people—are in contact with the child's unconscious, but there is still a difference between this and the understanding of the unconscious implied in psycho-analysis. (Klein, 100n)

In such moments, Klein is making a plea—one I would wish to endorse—for a more psychoanalytically attuned world.

So, in what, then, might the renewal of hope consist (which must be the only question)? At the end of a treatment whose long-term effects Klein is not in a position to predict, Richard begins to feel compassion for his enemies. We are on the last page: "He no longer felt impelled to turn away from destroyed objects but could experience compassion for them. . . . Richard, who so strongly hated the enemies threatening Britain's existence became capable of feeling compassion for a destroyed enemy" (Klein, 466). This too is a political as much as a psychic point. Before we dismiss it as unrealistic or sentimental (or both), we might remember that had the Allies felt sympathy for, and been less punitive towards, a defeated Germany after the First World War, we might not have witnessed the Second.

In her important essay on brotherhood and the law of war, Juliet Mitchell suggests there is an irreconcilable contradiction in how women are viewed in war.[10] They are both the defeated and protected—in double jeopardy, as we might say. Rape as a war crime would then belong at the opposite psychic pole to what Richard arrives at here. No compassion. Probably no recognition of what you have done. Certainly no place for your own dead objects inside your head. Instead, the enemy you have defeated has to be destroyed and degraded over and over again. On this, for me, Klein's bombed, damaged, pig-sty Mummy and Arendt's thoughtlessness belong together. Klein was no social commentator, but she has described a world that repeatedly condemns itself to violence and where women pay the price for men's self-blinding repudiation of the life of the mind.

To return, finally, to literary writing, which is where this essay began. Not to Plath and Sexton but to two modern-day women writers who I think bring what women can do with words, disturbingly, into its next phase, into our time where violence against women seems to have been raised to a new pitch. First Temsula Ao, then the Irish writer Eimear McBride, who shot to fame in 2014 with her UK Orange prize-winning novel, *A Girl Is a Half-formed Thing* (after her novel had languished unpublished for nine years).

Ao is Nagalese. She comes from that part of India that received the brunt of the newly independent's nation drive to crush anything that might tar the image of national unity in which it so needed to believe and project to the outside world. In fact, the Naga rebellion predated independence, as the Naga National Council was formed in 1946. The violence in Nagaland is not widely known. It is perhaps partly because Gandhi had stated that, after struggling for freedom, of course India would respect the desire for independence of any of its peoples, that the state then struck with such viciousness against the secessionist Nagalese.[11]

Ao entitles her collection of short stories, *These Hills Called Home: Stories from a War Zone*. She means it. She does not spare her reader. Neither of my two writers spare their readers—indeed not sparing the reader is the point, so this final turn to literature is not intended as a soft landing. As Ao states in her preface—"Lest we forget"—her aim is to probe how the atrocities of that era have "restructured or even 'revolutionised' the Naga psyche" (*x*).[12] Government forces would enter the villages with the intention to degrade, humiliate, and maim. In one story—"The Last Song"—a young girl, Apenyo, who starts singing almost from birth and becomes the lead soprano of her school, renowned across the land, carries on singing as a government soldier yanks her off to the local church where he and his fellow soldiers rape both her and her distraught mother and then kill them (Apenyo's song then echoes through the village for years as "one more Naga village weeps for her ravaged and ruined children" [33]).

The story I briefly focus on here is "An Old Man Remembers." It is for me one of the most courageous stories of the collection: first, for so boldly entering the life of a man's mind, and second, for what it finds there. Sashi is a man who has been part of the Nagalese resistance, although what he remembers is not a heroic struggle but a moment of violence which has haunted him ever since. The story is therefore a countermyth. It is also a talking cure. His aging body is racked with pain at least partly, the story suggests, because he cannot bring himself to tell the grandson who so lovingly tends him the truth about the war. "'Grandfather, is it true,' the little boy asks him, 'that you and grandfather Imli killed many people when you were in the jungle?'" (92). He is completely thrown, has never spoken about his jungle days: "It was as though that phase of his life was consigned to a dark place in his heart and would be buried with him when his time came. But now the question of a disturbed child stirred old spectres and left him speechless for a long time" (92). He has been hurled a question "from the other side of history" (93). When Sashi starts speaking, it is "like the massive gush of a waterfall which now threatened to drown both storyteller and listener" (97).

What matters is not so much the main incident he remembers and that brutally conveys "how youngsters like Imli and him were transformed into what they became in the jungle" (96). More crucial is the fact that the morning after, the young Sashi and Imli decide anxiously and hesitantly to go back to see what they had done in the night (they, and the reader, have to look at the one they have destroyed). Facing your own violence therefore provides the core of the story as well as its narrative frame. As the grandfather tells this story, he starts to weep. The young boy is baffled—"after all, they were enemy soldiers, weren't they?" (108). Why would you weep for your enemy? "Once in a lifetime," the grandfather says to the boy, "one ought to face the truth" (108). To portray the Nagalese resistance as the agents rather than the victims of violence goes against the grain of how this community, with more than slight justification, views itself—although for Temsula Ao, the future of her world depends on its doing so. "And the earth continued to be" are the last words of the story (113).

Finally, Eimear McBride. Commentaries have rightly focused on the form of the writing, above all on the shortness of the sentences, and the absence of the comma—although that is not quite accurate. There are commas, but they are used very sparingly and to dramatic effect. But the overall effect is of a voice starting and stopping, choking almost on its own breath, as in these now famous opening lines:

> For you. You'll soon. You'll give her name. In the stitches of her skin she'll wear your say. Mammy, me? Yes you. Bounce the bed, I'd say. I'd say

that's what you did. Then lay you down. They cut your round. Wait and
hour and day. (3)

The fact that we are, as we soon discover, inside the womb simply adds
to the suffocating effect. This is a voice—the only and unnamed voice
in McBride's novel—repeatedly halted in its tracks (a kind of breath-
lessness that places writing on the border between life and death). The
break-up of language and the more-or-less dismemberment of the
woman's body are inseparable (the language manages to be as unre-
strained and freewheeling as it is broken and clipped). It a story of
sexual abuse—by the uncle, and then, as we are later told, of the mother
by her own father: "Lie across each other's beds we tell each other
sorts of things. It makes us such close friends. No bits pieces left unsaid. And truth now tell the truth we say. Her father felt her up. It
makes her red and cry. Daddy still loves her the best but he wouldn't
want anyone else to try. That is love" (95). Abuse passes down the generations. Think back through the grandfathers, as, perverting Woolf,
one might say.

At the opposite pole from trauma as unspeakable, which is one
fashionable account of trauma, *A Girl Is a Half-Formed Thing* is trauma-
tized speech with no exit. "Out my mouth like a mad thing raving
clawing out my eyes" (162). As a reader you are given no cover. You
have nowhere else to go other than the narrator's head. Her brother
is dying—she has known this since before she was born (inside the
womb, where the novel begins). As a child, she is slapped, rammed,
bruised, and bloodied by her mother, who she also describes as her
"close friend" (95). Her uncle rapes her as a thirteen year old girl. She
responds with a form of crazed promiscuity that allows men, including the uncle, repeatedly to tear her to shreds. This is modernism as
slut walk, language as a type of syncopated abuse—the constant line
breakage as the literary form for injury or self-harm (as Anne Enright
put it in her review of the book, "You can almost hear the blows in the
rhythm of the words" [2013]). To take just one example—it is also a
rare sentence with commas: "I met a man. I met a man. I let him throw
me round the bed. And smoked, me, spliffs and choked my neck until
I said I was dead" (96). The fact that this can also be read as a nursery
rhyme simply intensifies the violence.

To take one moment from very near the end of the novel, her
beloved brother has just died. She walks out on the pious mourning

party of the gathered relatives and heads for the woods where she knows—she seeks it out—she will meet with a violent sexual encounter, one of a trail that have run through the novel but which, in terms of what it does to her, and to the language of the text, makes everything that has preceded it seem—almost—harmless. This passage, which is not the worst of it, comes after the encounter itself when, you could almost say, she is collecting herself:

> I lie thisright place for me with my fingers ripped onthebody Mine is Lie in the ground faceWhere I right for meyes. Think about your face. Something. Shush now. Right now. FullofslimeThere better now. And I am. Done with this done. Fill the air up. Smear the blood up is there any no no t reeeeelly. My work is. I've done my I should do. I've done the this time really well. And best of. It was the best of. How. Ready now. I'm screaming in the blackness. Scream up until I'm done my body. Full of nothing. Full of dirt the. I am. My I can. There there breath that. Where is your face off somewhere. Where am I lay down this tool. I fall I felled. I banged my face head I think. Time for somewhere. Isgoing home. (194)[13]

None of the first reviews and critics of this novel dwelled on the sexual violence at its core.[14] The moment will lead—more or less—to her drowning, which is how the novel ends. But note two things about this passage. First, the "you"—as almost constantly throughout the text—is her brother (from before her own birth till after his own death): "Think about your face." The destruction of herself is therefore her loving return to him and a form of care: "There there." This, incidentally, is why to describe this text as all interior monologue is not quite right. She is nearly always somehow speaking to him. Second, the narrator goes out looking for the violent encounter and knows where to find it. As well as everything else it monstrously is, it is also her achievement: "My work is. I've done my I should do. I've done this time really well. And best of it. It was the best of." Crucially, therefore, she is her own agent. Violence is sought. As well as being viciously what men do to her, it is a component of her grief. None of this mitigates anything; the protest against violence is not lessened but intensified. For me, the genius of McBride's novel is that she can get all of this onto the same page or line or word, into the strangulated syntax of her prose.

A Girl Is a Half-Formed Thing takes us back to where this essay started: to violence against women as the hallmark of the modern world. If McBride plunges us into the worst—and I have not conveyed the half of it—she also, like Sexton, like Plath, gives us a voice that brilliantly orchestrates its own sorrow and rage. The fight-back is in the words, in what a mind (the life of the mind, no less) can do with its own history. Along with the necessary fight for public and legal recognition of violence against women today, this continues to be, as I see it, one of women's best weapons against cruelty and injustice. As feminists, we do not have—should not be asked—to choose between the two, at least not in the world I want to live in.

Jacqueline Rose, critic, novelist, and theorist, is professor of humanities at the Birkbeck Institute for the Humanities, University of London. She writes widely about feminism, politics, psychoanalysis, and violence, and is internationally known for her work on literature, including authors such as Sylvia Plath and Marcel Proust, and urgent political issues such as the ideology of Zionism and the Israeli–Palestinian conflict. Among her many books are *Sexuality in the Field of Vision* (1986), *States of Fantasy* (1996), and *Women in Dark Times* (2014).

Notes

1. See Middlebrook.
2. For an account of these disputes, see Rose 2003.
3. Subsequently printed as Spivak 2015.
4. See European Union Agency for Fundamental Rights; Campbell.
5. See Martison.
6. See Benhabib; Dietz.
7. See Arendt 1970b; Rose 2014.
8. See Kristeva; Jacobs.
9. See Rose 1993.
10. See Mitchell.
11. See Luithui and Haskar.
12. My thanks to Akshi Singh for bringing Ao to my attention.
13. In the lecture this passage was not read by me but projected on a screen for the audience to read inside their heads.
14. For a fuller discussion of critical responses to the novel, including an account of the lecture in which I first discussed McBride—"Modernism: The Unfinished Legacy," delivered at the British Association for Modernist Studies (BAMS) on June 26, 2014—see Collard.

Works Cited

Ao, Temsula. 2006. *These Hills Called Home: Stories from a War Zone*. New Delhi: Zubaan, Kali for Women.

Arendt, Hannah. 1958. *The Human Condition*. Chicago: University of Chicago Press.

———. 1970a. *On Violence*. New York: Harcourt, Brace, Jovanovich.

———. 1970b. "Rosa Luxemburg: 1871–1919." In *Men in Dark Times*, 33–56. London: Jonathan Cape.

———. 1972. "Lying in Politics: Reflections on the Pentagon Papers." In *Crises of the Republic*, 1–48. New York: Harcourt, Brace, Jovanovich.

———. 1978. *The Life of the Mind*. 2 vols. New York: Harcourt.

Benhabib, Seyla. 1993. "Feminist Theory and Hannah Arendt's Concept of Public Space." *History of Human Sciences* 6, no. 2: 97–114.

Campbell, Beatrix. 2014. *The End of Equality: The Only Way is Women's Liberation*. Chicago: University of Chicago Press and Seagull.

Collard, David. 2016. *About a Girl: A Reader's Guide to Eimear McBride's "A Girl Is a Half-Formed Thing."* London: CB Editions.

Dietz, Mary G. 1994. "Hannah Arendt and Feminist Politics." In *Hannah Arendt: Critical Essays*. Ed. Lewis P. Hinchman and Sandra K. Hinchman, 231–60. Albany: State University of New York Press.

Enright, Anne. 2013. "Review of *A Girl Is a Half-Formed Thing* by Eimear McBride." *Guardian*, September 20.

Ettinger, Elzbieta. 1986. *Rosa Luxemburg: A Life*. Boston: Beacon.

European Union Agency for Fundamental Rights. 2014. "Violence against Women: An EU-Wide Survey." http://fra.europa.eu/en/publication/2014/violence-against-women-eu-wide-survey-main-results-report.

Jacques, Elliott. 1984. Foreword to *Narrative of a Child Analysis: The Conduct of the Psycho-Analysis of Children as Seen in the Treatment of a Ten-Year-Old Boy*, by Melanie Klein. London: Hogarth.

Jacobs, Amber. 2007. *Matricide: Myth, Psychoanalysis and the Law of the Mother*. New York: Columbia University Press.

Klein, Melanie. 1984. *Narrative of a Child Analysis: The Conduct of the Psycho-Analysis of Children as Seen in the Treatment of a Ten-Year-Old Boy*. London: Hogarth.

Kristeva, Julia. 2001. *Melanie Klein*. Trans. Ross Guberman. New York: Columbia University Press.

Lacan, Jacques. 2004. *The Four Fundamental Concepts of Psychoanalysis*. London: Karnac.

Luithui, Luingam, and Nandita Haskar. 1984. *Nagaland File: A Question of Human Rights*. Delhi: Lancer International.

MacKinnon, Catherine A. 1988. "Desire and Power." In *Feminism Unmodified: Discourses on Life and Law*, 46–62. Cambridge, Mass.: Harvard University Press.

———. 2006a. "Human Rights and Global Violence against Women." In *Are Women Human? and Other International Dialogues*, 28–33. Cambridge, Mass.: Harvard University Press.

———. 2006b. "Introduction: Women's Status, Men's States." In *Are Women Human? and Other International Dialogues*, 1–16. Cambridge, Mass.: Harvard University Press.

———. 2006c. "Women's September 11th: Rethinking the International Law of Conflict." In *Are Women Human? and Other International Dialogues*, 259–80. Cambridge, Mass.: Harvard University Press.

Martison, Jane. 2014. "Extent of Violence against Women in EU Revealed." *Guardian*, March 5.

McBride, Eimear. 2013. *A Girl Is a Half-Formed Thing*. Norwich: Galley Beggar Press.

Middlebrook, Diane Wood. 1991. *Anne Sexton: A Biography*. Boston: Houghton Mifflin.

Mitchell, Juliet. 2013. "The Law of the Mother: Sibling Trauma and the Brotherhood of War." *Canadian Journal of Psychoanalysis* 21, no. 1: 145–59.

Rose, Jacqueline. 1991. *The Haunting of Sylvia Plath*. London: Virago.

———. 1993. "War in the Nursery." In *Why War? Psychoanalysis, Politics and the Return to Melanie Klein*, 191–230. Oxford: Blackwell.

———. 2003. "'This Is Not a Biography.'" In *On Not Being Able to Sleep: Psychoanalysis in the Modern World,* 49–62. London: Chatto and Windus.

———. 2014. "Woman on the Verge of Revolution: Rosa Luxemburg." In *Women in Dark Times*. London: Bloomsbury.

Spivak, Gayatri Chakravorty. 2015. "Crimes of Identity." In *Juliet Mitchell and the Lateral Axis: Twenty-First-Century Psychoanalysis and Feminism*. Ed. Robbie Duschinsky and Susan Walker, 207–27. London: Macmillan.

THE JUDGE AS HISTORIAN
KNOWLEDGE AT THE LIMITS OF DOUBT (A RESPONSE TO JACQUELINE ROSE'S "FEMINISM AND THE ABOMINATION OF VIOLENCE")

Jane Blocker

On February 11, 1988, at 12:30 in the afternoon, New York state supreme court justice Alvin Schlesinger delivered his verdict in the murder trial of sculptor Carl Andre, who was accused of having thrown his wife, artist Ana Mendieta, out the window of their thirty-fourth-story New York apartment on September 8, 1985. "I have reached a verdict in this case," he said. "I have concluded that the evidence has not satisfied me beyond a reasonable doubt that the defendant is guilty" (Katz, 371). In the terms that Jacqueline Rose so beautifully lays out for us, we might say that Schlesinger's verdict was in fact a public admonition of the case set before him, which failed to accede to his "desire to know." The prosecution's case was weak and largely circumstantial: key physical evidence, inappropriately gathered, was excluded, and Carl and Ana were the only two in the apartment when it happened. She was dead and he wasn't saying, so knowledge was hard to come by. The judge's verdict thus passed sentence, not on Carl Andre, but on the case itself, which had not "satisfied," as he said, his doubt.

These two short sentences, uttered at the end of a three-year process in which the prosecution had indicted Andre three separate times before being granted a trial, along with Andre's own silence about the incident and refusal to testify, constitute an exercise of what Rose calls "false mastery," where mastery is understood to be the presumptuous claim made by knowledge.[1] The courtroom is, after all, a scene of knowledge (but perhaps not of thought), where the truth of "what happened" is sought and debated. In the absence of knowing, a condition called "reasonable doubt," mastery is troubled. "Violence," Rose writes, "is man's response to the fraudulence of his power and the limits of his knowledge." Unwilling to relinquish his own juridical power, precisely at that moment when it was most called into question, the judge committed an act of violence that wounds its victims to this day. The case is a perfect illustration of Rose's claim that violence against women is a form of "radical self-deceit—or 'the impotence of bigness' to use [Hannah Arendt's] phrase—which punishes the world, punishes women we can say, for the limitations of human power."

Of course the judge's violent act doesn't seem nearly as "big" as Andre's.

Before her death, Mendieta and Andre's nine-month marriage was on the rocks, and Mendieta, armed with evidence of her husband's infidelities, confided to a friend (Natalia Delgado) that she was going to seek a divorce (Katz, 319–20). It is not surprising that, at that moment, when his power was most threatened, she felt his explosive wrath. As studies on domestic violence repeatedly show, abusers are most dangerous at those moments where their victims seek escape. Of course, Andre's narrative of the events was rather different. According to the transcript of his 911 call, Ana had committed suicide. "What happened," he said, "What happened was we had—my wife is an artist and I'm an artist, and we had a quarrel about the fact that I was more, uh, exposed to the public than she was, and she went to the bedroom and I went after her and she went out of the window" (Katz, 11–12). The most chilling turn of phrase here is where he says "and I went after her." It was hard for me not to think about this violent death and subsequent trial when reading Jacqueline Rose's work, in part because of the recent exhibition at the University of Minnesota of some of Ana Mendieta's films, *Covered in Time and History: The Films of Ana Mendieta,* a show that was timed to coincide with the thirtieth anniversary of her death, and in part because of the huge retrospective exhibition of Carl Andre's work held at Dia:Beacon from May 2014 until March 2015.

The Andre retrospective was the first major show held in the United States since the artist's acquittal on second-degree murder charges. In the intervening years, he has primarily exhibited his work in Europe, where it is warmly received, in contrast to the rather cold response it has garnered from many in the New York art world. The show, in its "impotent bigness"—it was spread over six of Dia's vast galleries and contained over fifty works—was met with praise by many and outrage by some who still ache from the slap of the judge's ruling (Figure 1). It was also the site of two protest performances. Both were organized

Figure 1. Carl Andre, installation view from the exhibition *Carl Andre: Sculpture as Place, 1958–2010,* Dia:Beacon, Riggio Galleries, Beacon, New York. Art copyright Carl Andre/Licensed by VAGA, New York. Photograph by Bill Jacobson Studio, New York. Courtesy Dia Art Foundation, New York.

by the No Wave Performance Task Force, and the first took place outside the Dia Art Foundation in Chelsea in 2014 (Steinhauer). A small group of performers gathered (wearing white jumpsuits), taped a paper banner with the legend "We Wish Ana Mendieta Was Still Alive" to the sidewalk in front of the building, read from texts written by Mendieta, and then poured blood on the sidewalk (Steinhauer). The blood was part homage to the artist's repeated use of blood and viscera in her works and part grotesque reminder of the manner of her death. The other action was performed on the last day of the exhibition in Beacon, New York, where about fifteen women stood, knelt, or sat near Andre's sculptures and cried loudly and publicly, until they were escorted out of the building by museum guards (Crawford).

In answer to the horrific consequences of knowing, the consequences of what she variously terms self-deceit, fantasy, myth, self-blinding, and thoughtlessness, Rose proffers thought. "The best way," she argues, "for feminism to counter violence against women is to speak of, to stay and reckon with, the extraordinary, often painful, and mostly overlooked, range of what the human mind is capable of." "The fight-back," she says, against war, domestic violence, rape, and oppression, "is in the words, in what a mind—the life of the mind no less—

can do with its own history." With these particular examples of violence in mind, Rose has led me to wonder about whether it is possible to answer Mendieta's death and Judge Schlesinger's ruling with thought, or with what she calls a "complex internal reckoning," and how we can avoid seeing Mendieta (like Sylvia Plath and Anne Sexton before her) as the victim of her history.

When I first heard about the protests in New York, I'll admit I rolled my eyes in disdain. There has been something of a hysterical campaign (I use that word advisedly) to make Mendieta a martyr, to overidentify with her, and to revel in and speak on behalf of her victimization. On seeing the images of the Chelsea protest, I grew annoyed by what seemed to me to be a rather hastily thrown together and amateurishly performed action and by the ways in which it self-righteously claimed a feminist politics while at the same time leaving an unpleasant mess to be cleaned up by the powerless young women (part of the vast female underclass of the museum world) who work, volunteer, or intern at Dia.

The protest in Beacon seemed similarly silly—crocodile tears manufactured for the occasion by people who, judging from the photo documentation of the event, weren't even alive, let alone grieving, in 1985 when Ana Mendieta died. It's not that I object to the fakery—I'm a theorist of performance, after all, and have argued elsewhere that the line between the real and the acted is very hard to draw. Actually I would have been happier if it *had* all been a bit of theatre (an act of public mourning to make a thespian proud). Wailing, moaning, the rending of garments—the whole nine yards. But this? This struck me as a bit of self-deceit. Rather than being thoughtful, the protesters presumed already to know the truth of what happened ("beyond a reasonable doubt"), and they attempted to produce and make real their mastery by summoning real tears. I'm not sure if this even qualifies as "false mastery" since, as women, they have limited access to the subject position of the master, and since they employed that most obvious trope of femininity, tears. Thus I initially took the protest to be an example of the very kind of delusional fantasy against which Rose warns.

But Rose's paper shames me a bit and catches me out. The preface to my book on Mendieta ends with the clause "I did not know her" (xi). This is me dramatically throwing up my hands in feigned surrender to (and judgment of) the various groups that claim to have known the artist best, to speak for her—exiled Cubans, feminists, women of color, her teacher Hans Breder, her sister Raquel. But, as it turns out, this was not especially thoughtful on my part. I wish it were. I was playing a trump card: "I know (presumably unlike the rest of you) that I cannot know." The historian, like the judge, trades in evidence and fact, truth and doubt. In the short statement "I did not know her," I have rendered a damning epistemological verdict against the historical case of Ana Mendieta, an artist who died too young and who left an incomplete and contradictory archive; an artist about whom the evidence is wanting and the desire to know unsatisfied.

I am compelled, then, to take another look at the protest at Dia Beacon and ask whether tears (faked or not) constitute a form of thinking. Surely the act of crying suspends knowing, pauses the relation between self and other in a meditative gesture and physical expression of "thinking about." Indeed, this is how Marisa Crawford, one of the protest participants, describes her experience of public crying:

> I looked at an installation of metal squares placed in patterns and shapes along the floor. I thought about how women's emotions are policed in our culture. How Mendieta's powerful artwork—some of which features imagery challenging gendered hierarchies and violence against women— was used in court by Andre's lawyer to suggest she committed suicide. How prominent male artists of the time came to Andre's defense. How to this day we're all too eager to defend male artists who are abusers and to point fingers at women who are abused. (Crawford)

Her tears signal that she is suspended in the act of thinking—about feminine emotion, Mendieta's art, injustice, and violence against women. Strangely these hot tears (and the rage they express) oblige me to look again at Andre's work and consider whether, like Temsula Ao's story, it might be reappraised, renarrated as a countermyth or talking cure: all those carefully positioned metal plates, concrete blocks, Douglas fir timbers, and firebricks retold as memorials rather than industrial materials and minimalist forms; his work at Dia a vast graveyard in which all the markers refer again and again to the same death. Not Mendieta's death. Surely she has suffered enough at the hands of that story. Something else entirely—perhaps the death of knowing. In these terms, is there a way, following Rose's reading of Melanie Klein and Akshi Singh, to think about Andre himself as the victim rather than as the agent of violence? Is it possible that the tears shed at Dia Beacon were, in fact, shed for the enemy? I cannot know, and it is not for me to say. But the sickening squirm that such a thought produces is an indication of precisely how difficult it is to reject the image of the female victim, to reject the certitude and mastery of knowing, of judgment, despite its associations with masculine domination and violence.

Rather than press the women protesters into a narrative of forgiveness, I would do better to leave them to their grief and return to my own mythology. So I conclude these rather scattered thoughts with a question. How can I, as a historian (a judge, whose job it is to determine the truth of what happened in the past), engage in what Rose describes as "a form of memory which exerts no dominion, ousts no one from their own space, because it remembers that it is or once was radically homeless"?

Jane Blocker is professor of art history at the University of Minnesota. She is the author of *Becoming Past: History in Contemporary Art* (2015), *Seeing Witness: Visuality and the Ethics of Testimony* (2009), *What the Body Cost: Desire, History, and Performance* (2004), and *Where Is Ana Mendieta? Identity, Performativity, and Exile* (1999).

Notes

1. For information on the death of Ana Mendieta and the Andre trial, see Robert Katz, *Naked By the Window: The Fatal Marriage of Carl Andre and Ana Mendieta* (New York: The Atlantic Monthly Press, 1990).

Works Cited

Blocker, Jane. 1999. *Where Is Ana Mendieta? Identity, Performativity and Exile*. Durham: Duke University Press.

Crawford, Marisa. 2015. "Crying for Ana Mendieta at the Carl Andre Retrospective." *Hyperallergic*, March 10. http://hyperallergic.com/189315/crying-for-ana-mendieta-at-the-carl-andre-retrospective/.

Katz, Robert. 1990. *Naked by the Window: The Fatal Marriage of Carl Andre and Ana Mendieta*. New York: Atlantic Monthly Press.

Rose, Jacqueline. 2016. "Feminism and the Abomination of Violence." *Cultural Critique* 94 (Fall).

Steinhauer, Jillian. 2015. "Artists Protest Carl Andre Retrospective with Blood Outside of Dia:Chelsea." *Hyperallergic*, May 20. http://hyperallergic.com/127500/artists-protest-carl-andre-retrospective-with-blood-outside-of-diachelsea/.

CORPSING; OR, THE MATTER OF BLACK LIFE

David Marriott

CORPSING AND SOCIAL DEATH

The word "corpsing" (verb) signifies a blunder occurring when, in accordance with the performance of a role, an actor is "put out" of his part. A role that is corpsed is one that exposes the limits of performance and, depending on the metaphor, denotes the "death" of theater, as theater. A role that is corpsed, which is something contrary to the usual performance of a part, is one that evidently does away with an actor's mastery (of illusion) and no more clearly than when the disjoin between persona and part is exposed. Corpsing therefore raises the more general problem of how any kind of performance can proceed or withhold itself from the possibility of blunder when trying to follow certain rules, or at least how any performance that relies on the ability to properly communicate itself to another can do so without, conversely, also revealing that propriety as artificial and theatrical. For example, the fact that when an actor is corpsed he also reveals the necessary demise of their role, or what is most proper to its performance, it follows that the possibility of blunder—often hilariously— has a force and impetus that cannot be easily borne by the normal codes of performance, except in laughter. So too the fact that corpsing tends to produce a kind of infectious joy at the actor's expense, at his or her inability to subdue, or subordinate, the corpse (and its affects) to the governance of spectacle, authority, or ego.

But the fact that something so contagious should also compel an actor to give up his part and commit himself to a particular loss of character doesn't mean that we should lose sight of the fact that corpsing is also spectacle. And while I entirely agree that corpsing is usually determined rhetorically as a kind of excess of body over representation, I also insist that the whole scandal of corpsing (its impure force) lies in this spectacle of what happens when the most self-present mastery (of representation) comes across that which is both unmasterable and unrepresentable. First, insofar as corpsing reveals a discord, it is not clear from the metaphor whether corpsing denotes a failure to repress or the pleasure of failed repression, a pleasure that is also a death. Hence whatever follows from the failure of performance (that is, from performance itself insofar as we understand the corpse to be expressly, if unwittingly, performed) results also, albeit unconsciously, from the pleasures of failure. Hence the infectiousness of corpsing may quite correctly be said to follow from the spectacle of unmastering, because this spectacle depends especially on the failure of any resistance to manifest itself, insofar as the subject gives in to this failure but not without giving up on the persona of a role as I have just defined it. Second, I have said that this failure does not depend on decision or will but on the unconscious nature of performance, and a general consideration of accident and contingency cannot help us at all in the formation and ordering of particular corpsing events. For corpsing to be an event it must resist the very notion of event (i.e., as something ordered by the terms of performance, for it surpasses those terms). We are also ignorant of the actual motivations and reasons of why people corpse—that is, of why orderly forms of communication and performance succumb and fail, and therefore it is better and indeed necessary for what follows on corpsing and black social death to regard corpsing as radically contingent.

It seems to be only by a metaphor that the word "corpsing" is applied to acting and theater. What is commonly meant by corpsing is a moment by which an actor exceeds the limits of theater and no longer is in command of a role. Corpsing, therefore, seems to have been defined more precisely as the death of theatrical artifice. But corpsing is also evident outside theater; we see it when people fail to live up to or grasp their social roles. Hence the derisive laughter attached to those who forget themselves, or have their pretenses exposed, or fail to convince us of their authority. The promise of a role is meant to accord with the performance of desire, and corpsing occurs when desire violates or threatens that promise. In this way the codes of social performance are used to discipline desire like a bridle, insofar as one's persona is taken to be more than a formal tie of social being. This is why the essence of corpsing is the violation of rules of prescribed performance under the command of social laws, and consequently those who obey the rules are said to be at one with their roles and not regarded as subjects of them. But what if one's role is to be socially that of failure or if one is ordered and commanded to perform a role through one's corpse-like obliteration, would this not mean that corpsing can only occur when one refuses that spur and its contagious pleasure? Would this not be an example of a "death" of death, so to speak?

This is why the essence of the theory of black social death is taken to be a rule of life that prescribes to blacks that they live under the command of death (as citizens, parents, siblings, and subjects); consequently those who obey this rule are said to live under a law of symbolic death and are regarded as subjects who are already dead. So much about social death has to do with how rules of life are connected to the symbolically dead. What interests me here is how corpsing works in scenes of black social death.

Truly he whose role is to be socially dead because of the fears and hatreds of others is acting at the behest that his social life is lived always under the threat of suffering harm and of being corpsed the moment that he claims life; but he who lives as socially dead is given his due because he knows the true rationale of social life and understands its necessity, is acting at the behest of another's command of what it means to live (as black), and is therefore deserving of his role. I think this is what I was pointing out as a *fatal way of being alive* in my first book, and in my second, I compared the role of black social life to that of a revenant forced to live under a law of *revendication,* a word meaning both ownership and disfiguration.[1] For black social death, as it is commonly defined, is the constant and perilous exposure of life to injury, and this is why in *Haunted Life* I analyzed this as the relation between the ownership of black claims to be living and the performance of black life as a kind of epitaphic speech.

Since corpsing, accordingly, is nothing more than a rule for deciding when a role is accidentally, irreparably broken, it seems it has to be divided between proper and improper modes of performance. By "propriety" I mean the rule for those whose only purpose is to perform life as a kind of social death and to preserve life from their infection. By "impropriety" I mean the law that sees the socially dead not as a problem of truth or sensibility but of right and jurisdiction; that is, the relation of race to corpsing is one where the subject fails to escape its socially dead conception. The fact that something has left life but nonetheless returns and survives but can never be its former self raises the further question of the proper limit between right and interiority, or what separates the subject of right (in law) from his persona; between these two concentric terms (the one being *inside* the other) is assumed a reciprocal guarantee, which I will now explain as briefly and clearly as I can.

Since the best part of us is our social life, it is certain that, if we want to represent ourselves as subjects of right, we should try above all things to perform this right as the only guarantor of our jurisdiction; for our social being should consist in how well we perform the role. Furthermore, since this performed claim is always already marked by the fear of its deformation, which is the other meaning of "revendication," corpsing takes away all certainty and introduces doubt, and since we are in doubt that right is merely an accidental form of our being, it follows that right and perfection depend on illegitimate foundations. Again, since nothing can be absolutely performed or guaranteed without erring, it is certain that the more a subject's right to life involves and expresses a conception of life as right as its essence and perfection, the greater the risk of a failure and of a self-constitution without proper jurisdiction or sovereignty. Further (since knowledge of a role is no defense against its corpsing) the more we come to learn of our role (through the concept and intuition of right), the more we know that all performance is precarious; and all those rules—that is, rules of social interaction—not only depend on failure but consist in it altogether. This also follows from the fact that a subject is more perfect (and less abject) according to how further away he or she is from the merely mechanical nature of social obedience and therefore that man is most human and participates most in the proper realm of desire when he frees himself from a slavish obedience to the rules, which is where he is most vulnerable to the state of being corpsed.

This, then, is what corpsing is: the knowledge and loss of the rules determining the subject. But what of those subjects whose rule of life is to endure life under the ownership of another and consequently are said to live as objects and are regarded as subjects dead to law and who live in a state of permanent threat of injury? I think this condition of the slave is what the theory of social death is meant to explain and therefore deservedly calls attention to as a black state of exception. Therefore, race is the means by which corpsing comes to be a metaphor for social life, insofar as the slave fails to perform any juridical understanding of the subject as alive or sovereign, because it is perceived as having been born symbolically dead *(partus sequitur ventrem)* and therefore is reduced to an object, or res, whose prime value (if we define sovereignty as ownership) is a rule of life defined by its symbolic fungibility, which also denotes the end of life in terms of its reproducible nonexistence. It is this vision of corpsing as the natural life of the inhumanly alive (under cover of a logic of capital) that has led to both the reduction of black life to the fungible (in whose performance the owned life always arrives without a proper sense of life) as well as the fungible being seen as the foundation of an infectious laughter, which is where the trope of the dumb nigga begins (dumb in the sense of being unintelligible to law and language), thus marrying meaning with value in a way that is highly profitable and pleasurable. And because it is specifically as a corpse that blackness appears, blackness then assumes a fungible function, which many critics have well described as a form of social death. Suffice it to say, unlike the theatrical actor who consents to being "under" his role, it is evident that the socially dead do not arrogate to themselves the part or role they play in racial capital. Here I propose only to speak of corpsing in the context of social death in general.

Since the slave cannot easily play the role of a legal person—even when legal personality ironically refers to itself as enslaved it maintains the illusion of itself as formerly free—it follows that as society establishes, recognizes, and assumes the racial rights of citizenship, the black subject must confront the discomforting possibility that any performance of black social life is always corpsed by the fact that racial blackness is seen to be the performance of radical indebtedness or loss. The sum of black being, therefore, and its highest power is to know itself as a mortgaged claim on the living—that is, blacks must learn not to speak or perform life nor to desire this role. For the idea that black life can be rendered as a livable life that "matters" rather than a life lived in a state of injury or permanent nonexistence is to effectively transform it by corpsing the failed performance that blackness is. The white subject cannot understand this; it seems foolish to him because he has too meager a knowledge of what black life is and he finds nothing in black culture that he can refer to that makes any impression on his conviction that black flesh is only a thing he can take pleasure in owning or scorning, for knowledge of what it means to be black always takes the form of the following kind of existential reasoning: if he were black he would kill himself (because he would be already dead).[2] But those who know that they possess nothing more than life's refusal will certainly judge that being and right are the most unreal realities.

We have now explained what corpsing chiefly consists in and what racial corpsing is; for black existence has always been understood differently, as the sanctioned impropriety of right and being. For this too is how blackness grounds the metaphor of corpsing (as we have explained above), and in this sense black life does matter, even though it is not as life but in its preservation as social death, as confirmed by the historic law codes of racial slavery.

If we now consider the character of recent responses to blackness as I have just explained it, we shall see:

1. In the recent preponderance of extrajudicial killing, or the literal arrest of black life, the repeated performance of an "accidental" choking in which the relation of jurisdiction to propriety is key.

2. This does not require belief in any kind of right to life on the part of blacks. Since black social death is inferred from the consideration of black social life alone, it is certain that the spectacle in which the black body that suffers and helplessly succumbs is as much about confirming the proper role of blackness as it is about performing the sovereign power of whiteness. Belief in black social death, however pervasive it might be, can give us no knowledge of black life nor consequently of what it means for that life to become visible solely through its corpsing. For these murders are the expression of what Jared Sexton aptly calls "unbearable blackness," whose violent end must always be assumed; and so it is by no means the case that the belief in black social death is a necessary requirement for the violence of law to corpse the life it portends.[3] But although belief in such nonlife cannot give us a knowledge of black social life, we do not deny that antiblackness has a very useful purpose in civic life—namely, to decide who can and cannot live, where the

violence of law marks the limits of racial personation. The more we observe and understand the extrajudicial murder of blacks, which can best be seen as an unavoidable relation with injury or accident, the more we shall be able to see how blacks have struggled to maintain themselves beyond threat or injury and the better we shall be able to see how black life responds to its own deadly impersonation as the performance of a corpse.

3. We shall see that black social life is not disfigured by its corpsing. Corpsings are merely blunders indifferent in themselves and are infectious only by convention or those rules that represent the performance of authority. For black life to live itself beyond a form of death requires nothing but that it perform itself differently; it requires only what carries the clearest evidence of life's affirmation. For black life to go beyond the command of a tradition that relies on its symbolic representation-as-disfiguration, it must change the understanding of what it means to be black and living; it must change the way that it is seen as an infection whose dispatch produces intense enjoyment, so to speak, of body and mind. This also implies that it is in principle impossible to make sense of black life unless we posit what makes it unlivable, even though what gets corpsed is in a certain sense what keeps on living. We need not demonstrate all this here at greater length.

4. Finally, we see that the supreme reward of social death is to know the black law of fungibility—that is, to know that one's role can be endlessly impersonated whatever the complexity of the situation; the penalty of not knowing this is as fatal now as it ever was, especially when the gap that opens up between the ego and its enslavement by racist codes can legally be named as *dying while black*.

Having made these points, we must now ask: Can we conceive of blackness as a non-epitaphic discourse? If so, what kind of writing would that entail? What would it mean to make black life into a thing that matters? And lastly, what is this material afterlife that blackness seems to have won for itself in critical theory? I shall discuss the first two questions in the next section and the latter two in the final section.

POETRY; OR, THE RIGHT TO DEATH

What we should think regarding the first question is readily adduced from the movement known as Afro-pessimism, which is distinct in its analysis of black social life and social death; that is, the life alienated from life and subject to permanent dishonor are in reality one and the same thing in themselves and are only distinguished in relation to the codes of racist performance that inform them. That said, this emphasis on black symbolic death has proven to be controversial. For example, when we focus on criticisms of Afro-pessimism, we see a persistent tendency to link its analysis of black life with the phenomenon of nihilism and political pathology.[4] Proponents of Afro-pessimism are attacked for both an insufficiency and an excess of judgment, for being at once not black enough and all too predictably black in their reading. I've written elsewhere on why I think this is a peculiarly tendentious reading that, perhaps unwittingly, can only repeat the disavowal of blackness that they claim Afro-pessimism avows.[5] It is as if the act of saying that blackness has no value in the humanistic canon were the same thing as saying that the value of blackness is nothing; or as if measuring blackness against its denigration were to reject, dismiss, or pervert it. On the surface, of course, these accounts may appear to be reductive and inaccurate, but they are constitutive of a crisis in the meaning of blackness. Afro-pessimism refers to the attempt made by critics to include within the history of blackness (as well as its ongoing politics) more diverse questions and approaches than that offered by traditional cultural studies and identity politics.[6] Afro-pessimism is the name chosen by these critics to attack the ways in which modern blackness has been understood. For Afro-pessimist thinkers such as Jared Sexton and Frank Wilderson, among others, black life represents an ontological shift in the human. "Nothing in afro-pessimism suggests that there is no black (social) life," writes Sexton, "only that black life is not social life in the universe formed by the codes of state and civil society, of citizen and subject, of nation and culture, of people and place, of history and heritage, of all the things that colonial society has in common with the colonized, of all that capital has in common with labor—the modern world system" (Sexton 2011, 24). "Violence and captivity are the grammar and ghosts of our every gesture," says Wilderson, adding: "This is where performance meets ontology."[7] The choice of rhetoric in these two citations is no doubt interesting; both involve reference to racial slavery as a foundational event that, far from being over, is endlessly repeating; here, the social life of black social death acts as a kind of "index," or "grammar," that defines both the possibility *and* limit of black speech and existence. The phrase "where performance meets ontology" suggests that black social life can only be lived or thought about as a kind of debacle that, in turn, can only be performed as a corpsed remnant between the language and meaning of the human. No doubt this emphasis includes not only a certain, irreducible question of role and exposure but also one of responsibility and self-critique. In Afro-pessimism, however obscure its notion of social death may be, blackness is not so much claimed as performed differently so as to transform the philosophical question that blackness represents in both thought and politics.

If, for example, we were to compare Afro-pessimism to another key moment in black intellectual history—that of negritude, as set out in Aimé Césaire's famous *Cahier d'un retours au pays natal,* alongside various responses to this text—then we shall see another understanding of black performance as ontology; for Césaire's poem also contains reflections on corpsing's necessity and truth.[8] Based on contemporary accounts, Césaire's poem, no matter how initially obscure, seems to have been an ineradicable event in the *experience* of being black.[9] In this first major epic of the black experience, the caricatures of colonial life are transformed by a kind of deconstructive *questioning* of their absolute claims regarding historical and ethical life. The same holds true for black being itself: in the poem, the "natural" order of racial life is literally cut open by a single signifier, that of "negritude," whose status as a kind of radical autonomous act exceeds both meaning and judgment. As such, it is as a signifier arising out of nothing that negritude resuscitates what already considers itself socially dead. This signifier takes its stand, as it were, where racism grounds black being in a dead zone where black life and death mean nothing. Negritude thus becomes the bearer of a new performative; it speaks for those who lie *beyond* the petrification of blackness. Thus the poem has been seen as the outcome of a refusal that is also a resuscitation giving the socially dead new life. The enslaved dead have arrived—quite literally—from a time without us, from a past not our own, from a time that is not historical. As such, they denote the supernatural limit of what it means to be a *person*. Nameless, they arrive without sense or life; as augurs they are neither messianic nor miraculous. Because they come from a place that is literally dark—and here the middle passage is the metaphor of a primal dislocation—it has often been remarked that to try and represent or memorialize them one has to confront the discomforting possibility not of retrieval or of restoration but of having to read a text without the possibility of translation, one whose origin was seen as prior to history and language. The whole aesthetic of negritude in its achievements and promises was wholly based on the conviction (and the poetic proof) that these revenants not only allowed a grasp of the historical present but also made possible an act of authentic naming that is original and originating and one that dovetailed with a sacral, religious concept of black experience and history. These revenants were not so much given as claimed, split off from any location in history or narrative identity, they nonetheless signified the language of some original, mythic text, whose narrative identity suggested both political and existential possibility. In order to make the dead speak, reconstitute their ancestry, or redistribute their power—in short, to bring to light those who were made racially dark—negritude must annihilate or willfully extinguish (or, more generally, self-sacrifice) the present in order to invent a radically futural language: negritude would then be a *symbolon*, both symbol and what it symbolizes, whose naming harbors the promise of a revendication. That Jean-Paul Sartre, in his famous essay "Orphée Noir," refers to all these terms, as does Frantz Fanon in his 1952 response to Sartre, should come as no surprise here.[10] When Sartre describes negritude as an aesthetic, it is precisely because he sees something funereal and fantastic about it, something irreducibly mythical, since it is a sign of a transcendence that is unavoidable but unknowable. The opposition between himself and Fanon, as we shall see, will turn on this question of unknowability, which Fanon will insist is also untranslatable.

The main innovation of negritude, however—and it is here that we must modify our vision of it as performance—would be its descent into language as some kind of original and founding mythic violence. In order to purify language of antiblackness, the poet must recover other signifiers free of abjection (with the emphasis placed on the force of certain tropes rather than on their meaning). It is specifically this trope of forceful restoration and its phenomenological-existential vision that are often read as the superposition of an antiracist racism and one that is very specifically opposed to universal humanism. Whatever the validity of this doxa, the first thing negritude teaches us about blackness is not that it is an essence to be restored under the aspect of myth or natural creation but that it is just a signifier to be narrated or known as such, which seems to mean that negritude is not just another poetico-juridical personation of foundation (for the negritude text, be it Césaire's *Cahier* or, more recently, M. Nourbese-Philips's *Zong!,* is always articulated around juridical–historical codes it can neither actualize nor exhaust). In brief, the secret and sacral blackness that must be sought for and that underpins this hermeneutics proves to be just as illusory as the old signs of white privilege and hierarchy. This is a case of corpsing the whole history of racial parable and many of those narratives in which blackness is absolutely bereft and absolutely excluded from the white light of reason. Recently, rereading Césaire's *Cahier,* however, I was struck by how the pivotal scene on the tram brings to light—without reference to negritude or history—a poetic theory of blackness that shows the interplay of five different codes of corpsing: the comical, the ugly, the contagious, the shameful, and the symbolic. In this encounter with a poor, ugly, comical nigger, as Césaire presents it, what makes this man into a nigger is the racist laughter that demeans him, but what disarticulates the poet is his complicity with this laughter in his role as an imaginary white man.

> He was comical and ugly
> comical and ugly for sure
> I planted a smile of complicity
> My cowardly self rediscovered! (Césaire, 1995)

This complicity reveals a failure, an essential failure; from the perspective of a poetic language not yet entirely freed from the language of racism, we must necessarily infer that the encounter brings to light the negative affects that befall the poet in his shared racism, but there is no escape from the comical and ugly alienation that follows in its wake. This is how the trope of the *nègre* reveals a necessary truth about the roles we are asked to perform when those roles impose on us a particular alienation, a particular suffering, not from the nature of the action done but from the absolute pleasure and hateful complicity by which we corpse ourselves. Shame signifies exposure here; but the revelation is shattering because it signifies complicity with respect to racism that can neither be escaped nor borne and only because of the poet's cowardice via this knowledge.

It is for the same reason too (namely, his shameful complicity with racism) that Césaire evokes, in the final lines of the poem, the black abyss of language *(le grand trou noir)* to understand and so transform his mortification. Since the poem begins with the "old négritude . . . becoming a corpse"—that is, with the deadliness inhabiting its language—it ends with a new invocation: "And the great black hole wherein I longed to drown myself / . . . that's where I now long to fish out the / baleful tongue of night in its lustral stillness" (cited in Davis, 59). If the poet once perceived negritude not as life but as a social death to be rejected, at the end of the poem this same death is now embraced and performed differently. Why would Césaire speak of the poet as sacrificing himself to the great black hole of language? On this Césaire is very precise and offers us what amounts to an abyssal theory of negritude. What is meant by negritude, and the way in which its language means, is here radically different. The effect of racist language is not dialectical or historical, as Sartre presumes it to be, but *inhumanising*, and, more important, it opens onto a kind of unreadable rupture or fissure. For black self-liberation to take place, the equation of racist language with humanity is in question. What this means is that there is no racism necessarily in the way language means, for racism is not strictly a question of meaning, but one of performance.

For example, a word like *nègre* may be grasped as a performative, in the sense to which it decrees the thing it names by separating the mythically impure from what is seen as lawful and proper and in ways that compel obedience. When Césaire tells us that he grasped this complicity as cowardice, he is referring to the ways in which the word reveals to him how black being is literally corpsed by its own performance that follows on from how racial differences are somehow seen as real, embodied, or determined. Thus he perceived how language makes us complicit with prescribed racist rules and decrees. That is why at the end of the poem negritude emerges as a verb (rather than a noun), for it is about inaugurating black radical possibility rather than performing racist attributes and their lawful sovereignty. What is being named here as negritude is the disjunction between racist words and racial meaning, the former is the reason why blackness disappears, evanesces, and descends into an abyss, but the poet can no more escape or vanquish this abyss (this *trou*) or plot its emergence into historical meaning than he can prevent that sense from being corpsed, lost in a comical or ugly meaning. The irony that infuses this entire scene on the tram therefore suggests that negritude is at its blackest when it undoes any illusion of a black essence, which is, of course, the aim of all racist language.

I emphasize that these things must be seen as part of the history of negritude but that they are often overlooked. Hence we can no longer see the *Cahier* as Sartre saw it: as the expression of an anti-racist claim to history or as the dialectical resolution of both text and meaning. If negritude is a dialectic in the Hegelian sense, although Sartre appears to see this in Kojevean terms, one must see that the *Cahier* traverses various personae without resolution, via a kind of restless negativity. In "Orphée Noir," what Sartre calls the revolutionary nature of negritude is not so much due to its achieving that higher, more complex form of unity that is the universal, or its being the mouthpiece for a Marxist conception of form and its political–poetic history. For, as demonstrated above, the black hole turns form itself into a kind of radical contingency or accident without existential or political content (i.e., by means of performing anew the previous meanings of negritude as a corpse-like remnant). So it would be equally reductive to think that Césaire adapts this new role to suit his revolutionary political beliefs as that he previously adapted his performances of black alienation to racist belief (i.e., the belief that black life is a life not worth living) in order to communicate this revelation as the moment when his political restoration (as black) begins. No thought could be more absurd, especially as Sartre wants also to portray the black poet as the image of Orpheus sent to rescue humanity through an act of artistic self-murder. "I shall call this poetry 'Orphic,'" Sartre writes, "because the negro's tireless descent into himself makes me think of Orpheus going to claim Eurydice from Pluto" (121). It was not enough that blackness die; it was necessary that it should affirm itself as already dead—that is, that it should die in the universal and should reveal itself as transitory and delusional and limited in its conception and, like Eurydice, become ruinous when seen or touched, at "the moment that every black Orpheus most tightly embrace this Eurydice [their negritude], they feel her vanish from between their arms" (137).

Undoubtedly, since Eurydice never reveals herself to Orpheus directly but through intimations of love and loss, via imaginary words and visions, we can draw no other conclusion than that Orpheus's blunder is truly a corpsing event; for at the very moment he turns around to look at her, Sartre pictures him grasping negritude through its disappearance into universal words and visions.

Sartre therefore understood negritude as the desire for a self-renunciation that is also a generous surpassing. Hence "it is when Negritude renounces itself that it finds itself; it is when it accepts losing that it has won" (138). In this matter he suggests black life is a kind of wager that privileges losing as the only chance of winning; consequently, although he gave black poetry an authority and importance as political critique or philosophical history, he nevertheless still taught that blackness is a performance that condemns itself, especially when its claims to life beyond the false attributions of race can only end in death; the "twilight of his negritude . . . [in] the dawn of the universal" (138). To those who are capable of finding this dawn, he undoubtedly did see a future and not just a repetition; in this twilight both illusion and that which causes a break in illusion is what allows humanity to transcend, or repudiate, the false universalism of race. Hence he freed negritude from servitude to the law of racism and yet in this way also confirmed and stabilized that law, inscribing it deeply in black imagining. Particularly in the case of the politics of negritude, Sartre's analysis has been seen as reducing its political invention to "a certain affective attitude toward the world" (129). For Sartre, of course, what makes negritude revolutionary is precisely its historical, political transfiguration of art. It is in negritude's self-murder as art that its political restoration begins. This is why most readings of "Orphée Noir" are really posthumous readings of blackness as a voice-from-beyond-the-grave in its artistic and political necessity.

Sartre too seems to indicate as much in certain passages in which the loss of Eurydice is itself metaphorically lost *within* the dawn of a new Marxist history. While poetry names a truthful descent, only philosophy, it seems, can lead blackness to the path that opens onto a new beginning. As the self-sacrificing subject of negritude, Sartre says that the poet cannot simply expire; he must die a *racialized* death. If he fails to die as black, his death will not be dead enough. While, for Sartre, blackness/Eurydice is necessary to this ascesis, black poetry is always the posthumous work of its own demise. And though blacks will be reborn from this corpsing to enrich, poetically, the labored objectivity of liberty, they will still be symbolically dead in a double sense, drowning while trying to ford the gaps between black alienated life and its sublime transfiguration. The recognition that black social death can only in the end be *artful* once it has been redeemed as philosophy or politics eschews what I'm trying to get at here—that is, its abyssal undecidability. Similarly, Sartre's text does not stop at this allegory; he also says that the *situation* of negritude is due to a new revolutionary attitude toward language that is anything but abyssal. For Sartre, negritude is a prophetic style of writing, a *vates* or pathic use of thought and language that consequently resolves itself in *silence* rather than in logic or argumentation. It is because the oppressor's language is a "trap-covered ground" that black poetry, to escape this trap, must explode each word in its struggle for a complete *nudity* of French thought and language (123). Finally he says that, in contrast to the analytical tautness of French language, negritude must *"de-Frenchifize"* French in order to make out of it a "solemn, sacred superlanguage," whereby, undoubtedly, language is made into a sacramental object (123).

We conclude, therefore, that negritude for Sartre works as a negation (of racism) but remains trapped in the role of negation because, in this limited dialectic, the black poet seeks only the perfection of a "complete nudity" and so can never go beyond the sacrifice or holocaust of words (and in a way that misreads Bataille from whom this phrase is taken), within which French words are used precisely in order to dispense with them or at least to ceaselessly call into question language as such (124). Sartre's explanation of all of this is to say that literary form is merely a ruse, a mask (negritude remains the descent into the subject in order to bring back the subject as *vates*). And though we can't miss the teleological thrust here, Sartre's narrative is curiously prophetical in noting it (curious because *vates,* or "prophecy," is precisely the word he uses to define what is revolutionary about black surrealist poetry). He does not zoom in on blackness or single it out as a "situation," as he would typically do in his other work; instead he refers to negritude as a symbol of blacks *"becoming conscious"* and says that the poetry allows us to see this becoming and its passing from a (false) particularism to a true universal. The movement seems a bit diffuse, not pointed enough to justify the apparent point. A further, more pronounced indecisiveness may be observed when the Eurydice motif is used to reframe the politics and philosophy behind the poetry. Even as he isolates this figure at the edge of an absolute nudity, it moves back and forth with a tremor that makes the motion of going forward or back, up or down, oddly equivalent. The poet descends into an unknown region in order to drag us along in his fall. No doubt this descent reduces experience to pure affective ecstasy and is of value only to the person undergoing it. As soon as it falls under the sway of the dialectic an apotheosis occurs, the pathos loses its necessity, and the poem enters into its own death, as history. "It is the matter of making negritude pass from the immediate to the mediate, a matter of *thematizing* it," Sartre (125) writes. "The black must therefore die to white culture in order to be reborn with a black soul" (125). It is not in order to discover Eurydice's corpse as the black night of the world that negritude's self-undoing lies. As an instance of this sacrifice, Césaire's poetry must, in order to recover his black soul, refuse her, he must drown in his own desire in order to be marked as a subject of rebirth, only then will politics and art be radically transformed in their relation to the necessity of that sacrifice. That is why most readers of "Orphée Noir" say that Sartre gets the myth wrong; Orpheus is meant to find (through descent) and lose Eurydice (through ascent) precisely in order to discover poetry. In Sartre's version, Orpheus must do everything to refuse Eurydice (as symbol, as language) and so murder/rediscover himself in the name of a purer negation or eschewed negativity. Inversely, it is not until this suffering becomes historical that it reveals a certain *historicity* of meaning. It seems that it is only when the holocaust of words becomes historical that Sartre sees value in its poetic expression. This is why for Sartre blackness will always remain an epitaphic discourse.

Now let us pass to the second point, the stylistic choices running through the *Cahier*, to see what it shows us about negritude as black writing. The first thing that strikes us is that the descent from disillusion to poetry and politics is by way of a descent into a black abyss. Sartre presents this as an example of Orphic knowledge and metaphor. Césaire tells us, however, that the black abyss is where the symbol and what it represents do not correspond. The signifier "black" cannot simply be translated and precisely because it signifies an anamorphic limit to received ideas about loss and liberation. Fanon's chapter on

Césaire in *Peau noire, masques blancs* treats this disunity in a way that is strikingly prescient of Afro-pessimistic critique. First, Fanon is aware of the nondialectical meaning of the abyss (its structural role in the poem is not one of restoration but ellipsis). Second, his fidelity to the language of the text is his way of stating that black life matters precisely through its resistance to the authoritative ways of its reading. To say that blackness is singular in its difference does not mean that it does not contain its own imperatives and prohibitions but that its opacity (as a signifier) must nevertheless be maintained. What does opacity mean here, if not that the abyss is a signifier that cannot be translated? Is the black abyss a void or merely a plenitude that disguises itself as such? In any event, the abyss cannot void or destroy itself as a signifier, for to do so would be to erase its black materiality, to kill it dead. So that we can say that if negritude is a verb, it is very possible that its role is explorative rather than restorative, or that its logic is metonymic rather than metaphoric. Hence it is perhaps in that direction that one would need to pursue Fanon's study, to pursue his reading of the *Cahier*—its irony, not its truth. Evidently, there is a risk in so doing of weakening the identitarian claims of negritude (at the level of form and experience), but that is precisely Fanon's point. Yet equally in so saying this it is important to remember the Césairean tropes of descent that occur in *Peau noire, masques blancs* too. Descent invokes a movement that is not necessarily one of knowledge but one of fall or encounter. Indeed, Fanon addresses his introduction to those readers who lack the ability "to accomplish this descent into a real hell" and for whom an "authentic upheaval" is yet to begin (10). He wants them to descend "to a level where the categories of sense and nonsense are not yet invoked" (11). To read *Peau noire, masques blancs*, then, is to descend to an indeterminate place where the text situates its very *readability* as text; it is in this abyss that the reader will undergo a "fulguration" or upheaval (a word Fanon takes from Césaire) rather than a revendication. Therefore the distinction between revenant and revendication, the nonadequation of black life to politico-juridical reason, the unresolved character of this nonadequation, is Fanon's version of Césairean irony and indicates exactly the distance between this and a dialectical reading that reduces the problem of descent to a question of meaning or sense. Blackness is always displaced regarding its origin—that origin can never be reached. One is dealing here not with a naive romanticism but a constant struggle to displace the racist meaning of certain tropes as ever adequate to the meaning of black experience. This struggle is a corpsing, an irony, a permanent parabasis, if you wish, but it is not really the sign of an alienation, for there is no origin to be alienated from. Least of all is there some purity hidden by language or history, whose meaning awaits some *Aufhebung*.

It is better, therefore, to adduce negritude as a surpassing *through the depths* (with the ambiguity that that implies—the lowliest is the plateau from which the summit is built, and descent to the lowly is the role that must be left behind through ascent into the greater depths below: a leave taking from the lowliest into the lowest) only to find the lowliest returning to haunt the universal at the dialectical summit, and where *this* descent (the one that *returns* in an apparently higher position) is in fact the most abject performance. I mean that this paradoxically dialectical reversal (in Sartre's deduction that what comes last in the natural history of blackness really comes first) implies, with Sartre, that the really first revolutionary thing is not the apparently first thing, but also suggests, against Sartre, that no more is it the apparently last thing turning out to be really the first (history as the telos and therefore the summit of the most sovereign blackness). We will see how, as if reenacting this telos of death and suffering, Fanon causes negritude to appear like a Eurydice whose death is always *just beyond* death, the stage that also, then, turns out to be just *before* life, in a temporality that we can only guess at rather than make sense of "as the minor moment of a dialectical progression" (Sartre, 137).

BLACKNESS; OR, THE DEAD WOMAN

Black? *I felt as if the word were deflating, being emptied of its meaning.*

—Jean-Paul Sartre, Nausea

Man is a subject empty of errors.

—Aimé Césaire, "Poetry and Knowledge"

I showed in the previous section that negritude enacts a new role for blackness that necessarily has nothing to do with essentialism and everything to do with an abyssal explanation and consequently with a writing that inscribes a blackness of meaning deeply inside itself. We also deduced that role from Césaire's abyssal theory of language and, so to speak, the *Cahier* as its written performance. As for black writing, let these two epigraphs above stand as two different ways in which blackness can be written. The quotation from *Nausea* reveals the extent to which blackness can be reduced to an existential formulation. For the signifier "black" to *become* empty presupposes a fullness of meaning, but what Sartre's text actually performs is the meaninglessness of such projections. In enjoining the reader to watch the meaning of blackness disappear *within* the text and not to see it at once as the marker of its own disappearance *as* text, Sartre urges us to imagine the otherness of a world suddenly gone black. But in doing so, he absolutizes the authority of blackness as absolutely black, as the outlier to any code or reference. This is why, immediately following, the referent is not so much the word "black" but a world emptied *(vide)* of meaning by (black) structures of language. This also agrees with those passages from "Orphée Noir" cited above: blackness is always a *dark work* for Sartre, pregnant with its own expiration, and, in renouncing the nostalgia and desire to coincide with this Eurydice, black poetry can only establish its language in the void of her negation. In contrast, in the passage from "Poetry and Knowledge" we read: "Man is a subject empty *(vide)* of errors." One of the tenets of Césairean negritude seems to be that words such as "empty" are never empty as such and can only be emptied when deemed merely rhetorical, which is in itself an error of false completeness typifying the desire to be absolutely free of emptiness, or lack. In other words, if man is subject to error insofar as he tries to empty himself of lack, this error necessarily follows from trying to imagine a world of plenitude that he absolutely lacks. This ironic juxtaposition, which draws out the implications of what it might mean for a reader to respond to the *Cahier* as literally a *black* text, is also central to those scenes of reading as performance in Fanon and Sartre. Just as Sartre portrays negritude as "living like a woman who is born to die and who feels her own death even in the richest moments of her life," a "tragic beauty that can only find expression in poetry" (139), Fanon's response to "Orphée Noir" is to question this symmetry between social life and social death, or black life and suffering: "I felt that I had been robbed of my last chance," he complains (133).

Last chance? It is a phrase taken from Césaire's anticolonial masterpiece, *A Discourse on Colonialism* (1950), in a highly ironic passage on the opposition between a Europe devoted to racism (a Europe living under 'the mortal pall of darkness') and a Europe salvaged by "the only class that still has a universal mission, because it suffers in its flesh from all the wrongs of history": the proletariat.[11] From this quotation it becomes clear that Europe's last chance can be understood in two ways: either Europe recognizes those whose anticolonialism is allied to their Marxism or it admits that there is no possibility of its salvation. The later *Discourse* thus necessarily concludes that anticolonialism is a phenomenon that cannot be explained by European humanism and that it surpasses its understanding of modernity and enlightenment. Suffice it to say that this is not the same teleology that Fanon claims exudes an all-knowing disregard for the ways in which blackness *means*. Thus the universal mission of the colonial proletariat for Césaire is not the same trope as used in "Orphée Noir," for it comes into being out of something that must be understood clearly and distinctly as a particular experience of suffering. Consequently, a universal community is only universal insofar as it is bound by those particular experiences of suffering and is nothing more than the work of surpassing that defines the particularized agon of the colonized. I do not think that this vision is Sartre's, but it is clear that what is central to Fanon's reading of the *Cahier* is that the last chance should always come first, as the *black* implication of a poetic writing, before it is read as part of some Marxist–humanist orthodoxy, and so deemed merely historical. This is especially so where it is a matter of black life that is in question as a matter of *suffering flesh*.

As showed in the previous section, Fanon's reading of the *Cahier* is loosely organized around three propositions: that blackness is in some fundamental sense meaningless; that it can be understood as a void or unexplainable difference (the term is Bataille's) that absolutely resists cognitive knowledge; and that in some necessarily aporetic way negritude is nothing more than a substantively absolute difference that resists not only the narrative mastery of dialectic but also the prestige of the universal in white critical thought. I also deduced that negritude must itself be deemed as a void *(vide)* whose emptiness is irretrievable whether in the form of historical allegory or philosophical romanticism. It is certain, therefore, that although Fanon also sometimes criticizes negritude for being a romanticism in its belief that blackness offers an incontestably sacral or spiritual form of renewal (as in Senghor), it is also clear that his reading of the *Cahier* requires us to read otherwise. As does his critique of Sartre. Though the sway of Sartre's critique of negritude remains valid, it goes without saying that he loses sight of the relevance of such scenes as the tram scene in the *Cahier*. In his rush for the resolution of poetry in the truth of historical contradiction (which is, as already noted, the metanarrative of "Orphée Noir"), Sartre suppresses how Césaire empties the discourse of negritude of any positive content: negritude is *not*, Césaire tells us repeatedly; and even though he insists that it is not this and not that (neither a tower nor a cathedral, etc.), this has not prevented critics from trying to gain custody over what this not *is*. This principle of nonknowledge that gives the *Cahier* its rhythm and lack of resolution pushes beyond the limits of knowledge precisely because it is not grounded in revelation *or* negation, prophecy or myth, by conveying an emptiness that cannot be read or filled. I propose now to show that this insight remained central to Fanon. Then, for greater clarity, I show why and how Fanon, a former student of Césaire, remains a disciple of negritude in his effort to understand and work through its abyssal nonfoundationalism.

Fanon teaches nothing more clearly than that the *grand trou*—its danger and militancy—should not be reduced to history or aesthetics. In his response to "Orphée Noir," Fanon is concerned with the ways in which Sartre uses history to resolve and validate the meaning of the *grand trou* and in a way that excludes the aporetic self-questioning of the *Cahier*. When we read "The Lived Experience of the Black," in contrast, negritude is proclaimed as the effect of a certain linguistic predicament, summed up in these few points: the "n'est pas," or the not yet, that blackness signifies, and that I have commented on elsewhere, has no signifiable meaning, even though it continues to generate potentially fatal interpretive effects (2016). Equally important is the testimony of the *grand trou*: it traces a path that is without solution or synthesis; it figures a language (of blackness) that ceaselessly calls into question all origins but is neither a holocaust nor an offering. Thus, black life matters to Fanon only to the extent that it names this unknowable, utterly naked declivity, and excludes all meaning from it. In precisely this way negritude (it would be better from now on to say black *writing*) goes beyond a dialectic of interiority and substance (or secret and ultimate meaning) and instead ranges over a kind of unusable ascesis, one that is truly subversive since it refuses to embrace the corpse that blackness is in its meaningless exemption from reason, law, subject, or history. Other passages in Fanon's corpus testify to the same thing, but it is enough to refer to these two.

It is also evident from "The Lived Experience of the Black" that poiesis contributes nothing to *Aufhebung* and that allegory is only relevant to negritude insofar as it allows us to see it as an acute example of black romantic *irony*. Fanon makes this absolutely clear. In his reading of Césaire he demonstrates conclusively that nonsovereignty is the ambition of negritude, its texts being the affirmation of the life that is *not*, that has no existence, place or identity, as we noted above, other than this *néant*, or void, in which the black is obliged to lose or abandon himself as to an abyssal destination that cannot be represented or known and in whose abysses the subject encounters boundaries it cannot cross. If negritude is a battle lost as soon as it is waged, what Sartre failed to understand is that winning is not the point. On the contrary, as Fanon and Césaire repeatedly insist, negritude is a negativity emptied of content and is a mode not of praxis but of corpsing, endlessly and ironically, the racism of representation and not just the representation of race.

Equally, Fanon resists the urge to reread this irony as a form of teleological judgment. If he had wanted to give these poets moral instruction he could simply have followed Sartre, who advises these poets to wait for their knowledge to catch up with what white Marxists already know and for whom poetry is the act of an internal consent to being belated and so further proof that blackness must enter into the classic state of *ressentiment* in order to be taught the universal truths of Marxism. This is the reason why Fanon sees the spiritual reward of blackness as a falsehood of the most imaginary and abject kind; for Fanon, as I said, this obligation says more about white theory that, like a practiced magician or con artist, no sooner sees black experience than it instinctively begins correcting its posture, language, and speech. Hence, Fanon's overriding concern is not simply to bemoan the fact that Sartre's entire argument makes black Orpheus into a white philosopher—one who is wiser and more knowing—but to distinguish this reading from the actual working of the poetry. And so he writes: "And Sartre's mistake was not only to seek the source of the source but in a certain sense to block that source" (134). (Compare Sartre: "The black's secret is that the sources of his *existence* and the roots of Being are identical" [130].) Were black Orpheus to notice *this* oddity, it might be fatal to the whole enterprise of negritude. But if this source had been overlooked in his descent, and a white philosopher happened to observe it later, the only thing that would lose luster would be negritude's reputation as a discourse that returns to the essence of blackness (as to the "source"). Reset in this way, the most striking rhetorical feature of "Orphée Noir" is the decision to address Eurydice as if only a white philosopher can see her without loss: the conceptual "nudity" that such vision consists of renders her transparent to the white philosophical gaze precisely because white theory forgets the "absolute density" that structures blackness and that precedes any becoming: who then is Orpheus and who is abandoning whom to eternal night?

But let us return to our subject and offer other passages from Fanon's reading of negritude that calls into doubt racist history and, consequently, may be conceived as a refusal of an aesthetics of social death. No reader of negritude has taught this more clearly than Fanon. In the chapter of *Peau noire, masques blancs* condemning Sartre, Fanon commends the *Cahier* for not having blinded itself to the corpse-like nature of blackness and, in return, for not being seduced by the "truth" offered up by white politics or philosophy. Again, if Fanon insists that he "needed not to know" the endpoint of Sartre's critique, and if the reading of "Orphée noir" felt like the shattering of a "last illusion," what remains key for him is that we should not confuse the belief in negritude with the imaginary and prophetic vision of its blackness.

In "Orphée Noir" (as I have already mentioned), negritude is represented via the diurnal myth of Eurydice, in whose apparition the poet loses only to find himself both rhetorically and intellectually. Blacker than day, blacker than night, Eurydice's obscurity is inseparable from her promise, which can be seen as a kind of blinding flicker or absence of being—it is as such that Fanon encounters her in Sartre's text. On remarking on her first loss (of day to night), Fanon makes the pertinent observation that negritude itself is always waiting to find her, too; on remarking on the second loss, which requires a finer allegorical perception of poetry and philosophy, he remains uncertain of what he has *seen,* but he is sure that it was meant not to be *observed.* For Sartre seems not to need to give her a glance, let alone a thought, in order to justify her disappearance to philosophy. On the contrary, no sooner has he completed his reading of her portent than he is overwhelmed by a fresh burst of Marxist orthodoxy: he will serve the political superego on the side of whiteness, but the black body of Eurydice is not something he's prepared to look on. "Negritude is a sad myth full of hope, born of Evil and pregnant from future Good," he says, equating pregnancy with death, "living like a woman who is born to die and who feels her own death even in the richest moments of her life" (139). When it is said that negritude is also a prophecy pregnant with its own death, one could infer from this that its purpose is to corpse itself, or that it knows its role is to devote itself to its own death, but what it knows of this death as death is wholly philosophical.

Thus we see that revolutionary Marxism promises as the reward for liberating (the socially dead) Eurydice an improbable absolution "that knows it is transitory," and that condenses three different elements in Sartre's reading—the poem that is reborn as politics, the desire to become that fades into sacrificial nonexistence, and the corpse putrefying because, as Sartre says, it is "unamenable to analysis." And yet, in this gratifyingly obscure allegory of philosophy, Sartre concludes that any attempt to name or conceptualize black Eurydice philosophically is bound to fail, for only poetry can capture her "luminous night of unknowing" (139). All this evidently proves that, for the socially dead, the effect of being dead is both known and unknown to us and that it follows from the ordering of black being.

This, then, is what is explicitly the matter with black life: nowhere does it murder itself more than when it feels most alive, and nowhere is it most dead than when it relates to the living as a pious claim that it be allowed to come into being without the attribute of being already dead. It is no wonder then that Fanon should challenge this opinion as both symptomatic and foreclosed! Further, all these opinions of Sartre insist that negritude is solely a mythic understanding of black experience. It now occurs to me that my own reading of "Orphée Noir" in *Haunted Life* was perhaps too readily prepared to credit this myth of a black Eurydice. I may have been looking *too* closely at her and, in consequence of this fixation, find myself blinded—unseeing, dazzled—by the community of spectators who have confidently turned to philosophy to name or reveal Eurydice's meaning. In trying so hard to see her, to be the redeeming spectator, have I really done nothing but become a reader-celebrant of her loss? But no, not quite: after Fanon, who found himself walking both toward and away from her, it is clear that any reading of negritude is itself a revendication and one that shifts the entire argument about the limits of analysis; my observation is that this is key to his reading of negritude after all. It therefore comes as no surprise that Fanon, ever resistant to teleological narratives, should also resist the symbolism of a text as always already readable precisely in so far as it is unamenable to (white) analysis.

On the other hand, it is clear from her resistance to philosophy that negritude/Eurydice also prophesied this resistance: it is part of a logic of repetition that drives Fanon's response to Sartre but is also central to his reading of *le vécue Noir*. Faced with this insistence, let us briefly retrace what he says about experience in this chapter. What does Fanon say about *l'experience vécue Noir*? To my surprise, he refers not to experience but to loss and time: he thus begins with the motif of hemorrhaging. It is as if he were saying that after the encounter with racism the being of the (white-identified) black *empties* itself *(vide)*. "I *needed* not to know," he writes, implying that this new "decline" has yet to take on the formal aspect of "completeness" (135). Fanon's reading of Césaire's poetry confirms the same thing; for as we said, the abyss cannot be defined as completeness and its language abolishes the role of myth as superfluous to its meaning. What's more, the poetic and linguistic emphases of this poem—those that had formed the very standard against which Sartre perceives that Césaire "realizes" the "great surrealist tradition" (Sartre, 128)— begin to hemorrhage with their irregular reading of blackness as performance: whether as myth or negativity, "natural eros" or revolutionary poetry, the *Cahier* signifies a date in the *poeticization* of being black. It is as though Fanon had craftily acknowledged this date, which, having arrived on the road of destiny the moment he came across it, could never be removed *as* poetry, and so has to disappear as racial myth.

These passages, I think, support my position regarding Fanon's three most innovative responses to Césaire, as already mentioned above. I have more to say about these later on, but first I want to discuss the politics that Fanon's rearward glimpse back towards the *Cahier* signifies on the other side, as it were, of negritude. The oblivious need not to know is just where the first discovery leaves him, resetting the terms of the journey to his negritude. Fanon starts out on that journey as a search for meaning where, as a pretext for the new discovery of negritude, it is to be laid out for easy perusal by Césaire's poetic epic. As he is doing this, he sees—like every other spectator—negritude as a chimera just dangling out of reach, and, like these other readers, he waits for the world to notice it too. But at nearly the same moment— in this, *not* like the negritude philosopher—he again catches sight of negritude as not a "remarkable discovery"; indeed, this brief glimpse suffices to tell him that, since he first saw it, "this discovery was a rediscovery" (130). The "limits of my essence," he writes, has been turned into a sign of belatedness, and negritude, formerly occupying the leftmost (or hindmost) fecundity of the world, now stands exposed as the "zero" that he first imagined it to be. By virtue of this reversal, negritude confirms Sartre's reading of it as black unhappy consciousness: it is out of place and time in *two* ways now. It remains now to show how and why Fanon's disillusion with negritude nonetheless serves to preserve and maintain it as a most radical form of corpsing. I shall demonstrate this through one telling example: that of experience.

Anyone reading *Peau noire, masques blancs* must, in order to understand it, confront Fanon's concept of experience. That is, one must come to terms with the persona or masks by which whites convince themselves of their whiteness by becoming unwittingly black and blacks learn to perform themselves as white through an unconscious fear of their own blackness. However, unless these experiences are understood as imaginary misrecognitions, they will, even though it might be convincing to say so, still not suffice to illustrate Fanon's understanding of the word "experience," especially where it is a matter of questioning roles that put in question, or corpse, what is often meant by the term. Often though, a long chain of linked inferences is required to follow the intellectual argument that connects persona to phobia, phobia to what Fanon calls "that within," a phrase that he takes directly from theater, where it is linked to the role played by unconscious ambivalence in the constitution of the racist subject. Furthermore, this requires great caution and perspicacity regarding Fanon's understanding of psychoanalysis in the dramas of racism. Critics tend to read Fanon's concept of experience as if it were just an existentialist premise of self-alienation, or inauthenticity. Consequently, when the performance of racism is at issue, not to speak of the entire question of unconscious desire, critics often lose sight of the inferences linking his arguments together—especially the way in which he substantiates his points about experience through the definition of "that within."

For example, when he refers to his case histories of negrophobia—that is, when he's trying to explain how certain interracial fantasies require certain personae and narratives (namely, stories of rape and black rapists)—Fanon is anxious to point out that these personae and testimonies always involve a kind of unconscious corpsing through which the ego violates itself and for whom that violation can be enjoyed through the pleasures of failed repression (as can be seen in the infamous case history of "a Negro is raping me"). The purpose of the fantasy, in brief, is to allow a violation in which the subject does nothing at his own discretion and everything at the command of the black other, except that the ego's obeyance to commands prescribed by race law is what allows both the fantasy of obedience and its sadism (and here the black is obliged to symbolize both the aggressor and the injured, both legislator and victim of law) to be continually enjoyed without consequence.

From all this it is clear that what connects "that within" to the performance of interracial desire is the psychical benefits of corpsing, and consequently it has nothing to do with the existential rhetoric of inauthenticity. Concerning that rhetoric and its notion of authentic and inauthentic experience, it would be a mistake to understand "that within" as an example of bad faith. As I recognize it, Sartre's example of bad faith always means people are in denial about the choices they make and especially when their lives are bound to them. Indeed, one could almost say that Sartre, insofar as he is always obliged to point out what these choices might mean, is always able to decide what living the good life consists of and, in so doing, actually proves the point by making the example of bad faith the pious sign of a critical faith but not the bad faith of his own philosophical reading, related to the certainty that he knows and consequently never doubts this reading. Manifestly intelligible, controlled, and exempt from any symptom of self-doubt or uncertainty, Sartre's style appears nearer mastery and perfection the further it gets from experience; and we never feel better as readers of Sartre than in recognizing how each instance of authenticity is confirmed and each principle of bad faith traduced. By contrast, Fanon's style (of which I take the chapter on le vécue Noir as a key example) is aphoristic, recessive, poetic, esoteric, and hard to see, much less sum up. Like some faintly transmitted white ectoplasm, it can only reach those unhappy few who (by dint of pathology, bad luck, elective affinity) attend to the text precisely in order to see themselves reflected there. To see themselves in close-up, I mean, for the comfort of aesthetic appreciation, since the Fanonian style, invariably linked to the various symptoms, oversights, and inelegancies that run all through the text, seems to treat no other subject but *the failure of the black to be recognized or seen* beyond the symbolism of its corpsing. Sartre's compulsive aesthetization of negritude would receive its dialectical correction in Fanon's resistance to theory's aesthetic racialization of black experience as always already comprehended by the "life" of a concept.

Therefore, since all of those scenes of "that within" are revealed for the benefit of showing how racism is performed and, ultimately, enjoyed, the notion has considerable repercussions for Fanon's views on experience. Let us explain this more clearly. Among the many neurotic obsessions of the patients that Fanon presents, the most important is that of sexual difference, or rather white and black women whose ambivalence toward black men is seen as both the greatest punishment as well as the last chance of "authentic love" (a phrase laced with deep irony). These obsessions are too coherent *as* structures not to be symptoms, but they are so deviously concealed that, once they are observed, the ostensible story is lost to view. Like Eurydice in Sartre's "Orphée Noir," these negrophobic women are hidden, remarkably out of place to the experiences they are used to narrate, but they must also be *seen* to be impossibly out of place, unable to yield or teach any clear knowledge but who illumine the truth of desire precisely because of their obscurity. With this ghostly Eurydice, Fanon employs one of his favorite forms (the perverse *inform*) but empties it of its customary consequence; this figure sheds no other light but the obscure brilliance of its perverse elaboration of white–black desire.

From this I think it is clear that "that within," which for Sartre is among the ways in which an actor comes to play a role in bad faith and who takes pleasure in being dispossessed by this part, is the frame through which Fanon interrogates the limits of black existence or, more accurately, black existence *as* art. Even in the framing that finally makes such experience appear, it is not the only thing that we see. Those who have read those chapters in *Peau noire, masques blancs* dealing with sexuality will have earlier observed that, in denying that he has anything to say about homosexuality, for example, or black women ("I have nothing to say about her"), Fanon leaves these corpses sticking up out of the text. Now that once unruly, inauthentic desires have been fastidiously turned down, why is it that there is no evidence of "authentic love" to oppose this? They will further notice, along with black and white women, a third figure in need of (failed) repression: the black neurotic who can only reject the role that racism imposes on him by abandoning himself as living, as expressed above, and who also possesses a drive (rather than a desire) to be socially dead. Jean Veneuse is Fanon's main example here, who is the case of someone who believes that to be black is to be dead and who is driven to mourn this fact by calling off his love affair with a white woman (for it follows that if she loves him she is not competent to perceive clearly and distinctly the difference between life and death, or how black life sustains itself as already dead). Crossing over from desire to discourse, from loss to its memorialization, black existence becomes spectral here; and in repairing Veneuse's oversights, Fanon also comes to resemble him in making gaffes of his own, fouling up the neurotic force of "that within" that is *Un homme pariel aux autre's* obvious formal ideal. But with, as mentioned above, this crucial disparity—unlike Sartre say, who never notices his oversights (the romanticism, the philosophy, even, in the end, the teleology)—Fanon often seems to bestow on his own lapses a strange, secret *assent* (that requires the ambivalent refusal of negritude). To prove his doctrine that "that within" is a thoroughly neurotic structure, Fanon insists that it is impossible to draw the conclusion that Veneuse's neuroses are a symptom of his blackness, despite obviously demonstrating their derivation from experiences of black social death. Why should he simultaneously attend to feelings of being dead and yet deny the circumstances and histories from which those feelings derive? I remain unpersuaded that this is simply due to the masculinism of Fanon's own text, and much less do I believe that this is due to a blunder, or corpsing, of his reading of psychoanalysis, or a failure on Fanon's part to comprehend the classically triadic narrative structure of loss, recovery, and loss again by which Veneuse imagines himself to be the loss that loses itself, infinitely, in *Un homme pariel aux autre*. In disclosing an essentially faulty, flimsy, transient negritude, Fanon seems to be performing a role instructively linked to a broader—and undeniably controversial—failure of judgment, since here he gets more pleasure from corpsing that demonstration than from critiquing the actual doctrine of blacks having to mourn their failure to make a claim on the living. What is less known (or studied, perhaps) is how this inversion turns on a different reading of phobic neuroses in Fanon's final, posthumous work. But that is another story that I have written about elsewhere (2007; forthcoming).

What can be said about this disillusion with disillusion at the level of theory? To remove blackness from myth is extremely useful, indeed wholly essential, not only for severing blackness from its fetish but also for understanding black social being separately from its performance. For unless we are willing to see blackness as real and not just as a phantasm, we will be unable to distinguish its imaginary role from its real historical significance. We should add, though, that when we say that an awareness of their difference is necessary, we do not mean awareness of literally how one stands apart from the other but rather how one radically informs the other, which is one of Fanon's most important insights. For if performance is ontology, and it were impossible to know blackness without a thorough consideration of all its roles and performances, then obviously the demonstration and derivation of fantasy from the real, and vice versa, would allow us to grasp the ways in which blacks are put out of their roles not just neurotically, politically, or historically, but aporetically too. In Fanon's version of negritude, blackness is neither the coming of a plenitude nor a posthumous self-erasure, nor is it merely the reversed turn under the glimpse of theory to authenticity, not to mention the redemptive capacity of a no-win wager, which is then seen as a timely victory for those positioned precariously at the dawn of history. Again, let us state the conclusion we set out to prove, namely that, whatever the validity of Fanon's reading of the *Cahier,* he is not concerned to spell out its dialectic, nor does he wish to prove that some forms of blackness are more important than others or that poetry is subservient to philosophy. No, the only reason he reads the *Cahier* is to explain how certain roles inevitably corpse their actants and how certain acts, albeit completely ignorant of their being corpsed, are nevertheless salutary in offering blacks a new conception of living, beyond the common wretchedness, neuroses, and social dishonor.

However, white existential philosophy holds completely to the opposite view. Sartre thinks that a black conception of life makes no contribution to the universal *as* black, and so he spells out its dialectic and lets its ending be known, as transient. This prophesizing leads him to openly assert that blackness has only one chance: to corpse itself as a failed negritude, which has been cleansed and denuded for the purpose. Throughout all this, the black seems not to breathe until philosophy puts the black life of social death back into the underworld that defines him. And to Fanon's utter chagrin after Sartre does this, negritude, praised as an aesthetic of sacrificial generosity, finally looks acceptable. Moreover, with negritude again banished to the edge of the frame, poetry succumbs to the same back-and-forth tremor of what Fanon calls the "nonexistent" (the aesthetic equivalent of the idea of black existence as a stutter between nothingness and infinity) that he accuses Sartre of plunging him back into. The symmetry suggests a tragic denouement; a sequence has been concluded, a chiasm rounded out, a glimpse that is loss itself finally seen for what it is as a judgment that is forever and without any way of escape, with theory in charge of bringing this black essence to life. I think it is evident to anyone who reads *Peau noire, masques blancs* attentively that all this is treated as mere projection and does not rest on the authority of black experience, and hence one need only expound it in order to refute it.

I would add just this, if we can show on the basis of these texts that black death can never be sovereignly dead, nor entirely alive (which would come to the same thing)—what are we to make of this life-death? Historically we must never forget, of course, blackness is always caught up in the catastrophe that this endless death harbors. This is death as nothing, less than nothing; as such, this death is never assumable as possibility. But if this death is perturbing, it does not perturb us more than those attempts to sublate it as a deformation that keeps on living as, for example, the perpetual fall or descent into an abyssal insignificance (the minor term defining a transcendental crossing). There is no debate to be had here, insofar as the choice must presuppose two roles: in one, the black realizes his abject complicity with illusion; in the other, he is always the victim of a murderous disillusion against which he is too stifled or feeble to defend. Nothing, not even his death, drives away this drive to corpse himself as both possibility and representation. Likewise, the Orphic (white) reader, through always at the frontier of that self-mortification, cannot look back on it without losing it, or providing the last redemptive act that is also its murder. I hope and trust, to that extent, that if black life matters, it cannot be as a revendication, nor as the poetical grasp of a historical meaning, nor as the breathless emergence of a politics of ascent. For such roles are not meant for the living; they depend on the idea that blacks can only perform and perfect the role of their deaths, and that they should do so forever.

David Marriott teaches at the University of California, Santa Cruz. He is the author of *In Neuter* (2014), *The Bloods* (2011), and *Haunted Life* (2007). *Whither Fanon? Studies in Caribbean Culture and Philosophy* is forthcoming from Stanford University Press.

Notes

1. Marriott 2000, 15; 2007.
2. The word "nigger" in an absolute sense signifies either a drive to life and pleasure that acknowledges itself as contrary to law or, in the same fixed and determined way, a form of life that is also the performance of a kind of death, as in the trope "If I were a nigger, I would kill myself." In both instances, blackness is taken to be a role that is at odds with life itself, or is aberrant regarding right, life, and value.
3. Sexton 2015, 173.
4. For example, see Moten; and for a response, see Sexton 2011.
5. Marriott, "Judging Fanon," *Rhizomes*, forthcoming.
6. See Wilderson 2010; Sexton 2008; Han 2015; Sharpe; Keeling.
7. Wilderson 2009, 123.
8. The literature on negritude and Césaire's poem is vast, but see in particular Davis; Edwards; Nesbitt; Jones; Bernasconi.
9. See Breton.
10. See Sartre; Fanon.
11. Césaire 2001, 78.

Works Cited

Bernasconi, Robert. 2002. "The Assumption of Negritude: Aimé Césaire, Frantz Fanon, and the Vicious Circle of Racial Politics." *Parallax* 8, no. 2: 69–83.

Breton, André. 2008. *Martinique: Snake Charmer*. Trans. David W. Seaman. Austin: University of Texas Press.

Césaire, Aimé. 1995. *Notebook of a Return to My Native Land*. Trans. Mirielle Rosello and Annie Pritchard. Durham: Bloodaxe Books.

————. 2001. *Discourse on Colonialism*. Trans. Joan Pinkham. New York: Monthly Review Press.

Davis, Gregson. 1997. *Aimé Césaire*. Cambridge: Cambridge University Press.

Edwards, Brent. 2005. "Aimé Césaire: The Syntax of Influence." *Research in African Literatures* 36, no. 2: 1–18.

Fanon, Frantz. 1967. *Black Skin, White Masks*. Trans. C. L. Markmann. New York: Grove Press.

Han, Sora. 2015. *Letters of the Law: Race and the Fantasy of Colorblindness in American Law*. Stanford: Stanford University Press.

Jones, Donna V. 2013. *The Racial Discourses of Life Philosophy: Negritude, Vitalism, and Modernity*. New York: Columbia University Press.

Keeling, Kara. 2007. *The Witch's Flight: The Cinematic, the Black Femme, and the Image of Common Sense*. Durham: Duke University Press.

Marriott, David. 2000. *On Black Men*. New York: Columbia University Press.

————. 2007. *Haunted Life: Visual Culture and Black Modernity*. New Brunswick: Rutgers University Press.

————. Forthcoming. "Judging Fanon." *Rhizomes* 28.

Moten, Fred. 2008. "The Case of Blackness." *Criticism* 50, no. 2: 177–218.

Nesbitt, Nick. 2003. *Voicing Memory: History and Subjectivity in French Caribbean Literature*. Charlottesville: University of Virginia Press.

Philip, M. NourbeSe. 2008. *Zong! As Told to the Author by Setaey Adamu Boateng*. Middletown, Conn.: Wesleyan University Press.

Sartre, Jean-Paul. 2001. "Black Orpheus." In *Race* . Ed. Robert Bernasconi, 115–43. Trans. J. MacCombie. Oxford: Blackwell.

Sexton, Jared. 2008. *Amalgamation Schemes: Antiblackness and the Critique of Multiracialism*. Minneapolis: University of Minnesota Press.

————. 2011. "The Social Life of Social Death: On Afro-Pessimism and Black Optimism." *InTensions* 5 (Fall/Winter): 1–47.

————. 2015. "Unbearable Blackness." *Cultural Critique* 90 (Spring): 159–78.

Sharpe, Christina. 2010. *Monstrous Intimacies: Making Post-Slavery Subjects*. Durham: Duke University Press.

Wilderson, Frank. 2009. "Grammar and Ghosts: The Performative Limits of African Freedom." *Theater Survey* 50, no. 1: 1119–25.

————. 2010. *Red, White & Black: Cinema and the Structure of U.S. Antagonisms*. Durham: Duke University Press.

MASKING
(A RESPONSE TO DAVID MARRIOTT'S "CORPSING; OR, THE MATTER OF BLACK LIFE")

Paula Rabinowitz

> For black life to live itself beyond a form of death requires nothing but that it perform itself differently; it requires only what carries the clearest evidence of life's affirmation.
>
> —David Marriott

> At certain moments, the black man is locked in his body. . . . The real leap consists of introducing invention into life.
>
> —Frantz Fanon, Black Skin, White Masks

I am most grateful to David Marriott for his powerfully evocative and eloquent ruminations on "The Matter of Black Life."[1] My comments cannot do justice to its beautiful and ironic trill, which resonates in deep and complex ways with Jacqueline Rose's essay on violence against women. Rose connects political structures to psychic ones via Hannah Arendt and Melanie Klein, and begins with a meditation on two major postwar U.S. women poets, both suicides, Anne Sexton and Sylvia Plath, concluding with two contemporary works of postcolonial and working-class women's fiction, Eimear McBride's *A Girl Is a Half-Formed Thing* and Temsula Ao's *These Hills Called Home: Stories from a War Zone*. As such, Rose turns our attention to literature as the means for piercing surface matter.

David Marriott extends this concern with language and poiesis, this focus on politics and psychoanalysis, by paying attention to the full import of simple declarative sentences. The original talk out of which this essay emerged—entitled "Corpsing"[2]—began with the last words of Eric Garner in Staten Island, New York, "I can't breathe," and Jimmy Mubenga in London, "They're killing me." As such, "Corpsing" centers on the current political actions of Black Lives Matter by focusing on the series of three short words, both uttered with a colloquial contraction, comprising each phrase. The final words of Garner and Mubenga link the selves of those being choked and restrained to their anticipated deaths ("I can't breathe"—I am already dead, a corpse; "They're killing me"—I am in the process of dying, becoming a corpse)—and also the collective resistant stance against these sanctioned isolated murders of black men by representatives of the state: BLACK LIVES MATTER. But Marriott want us to see more: Black lives are matter, are the matter at hand, and the pressing question for our time: how to stop racist violence from destroying lives, lives lived as black lives—that is, as lives that must be so named and thus lived as such because of white racism. This is the state of things here and now. How, Marriott asks, echoing W. E. B. Du Bois, does it feel to be not only "a problem" (or, echoing Zora Neale Hurston, a "colored me"?) to be corpsed—ghosted, even as live matter—at this point, still, in the twenty-first century?

Marriott's intricate argument connects scenes of violence, specifically violence perpetrated against black men by state actors—that is, the police (who, at one point, James Comey, director of the FBI, noted, were being constrained by the so-called Ferguson effect, causing murder rates to climb [Schmidt and Apuzzo])—along with the words uttered during the attack by the victims (future corpses) to the performative interruption of corpsing. These dying black men's words, reverberating across the planet, rehearsed and reuttered (like the words spoken in a play) by those still living, call attention to the already damaged life, the already dead life, entailed in what Orlando Patterson named social death: "Black life *is* itself this deadly personation," Marriott had commented at the symposium. But not quite. And this is the substance of his essay—to make trouble, to raise the dead, and so ask again: what is the matter? How can a life lived, in a state of injury or permanent nonexistence, effectively transform itself without reflecting on the terms of its own death? Pondering this, to begin to answer this pressing question of today, he returns us, no, not to the source, but yes, to the source, to the discourse and source: to the decades immediately after World War II—to Aimé Césaire, to Jean-Paul Sartre, to Frantz Fanon and the debates about negritude, poetry, and black consciousness in the aftermath of war and the emergence of struggles for decolonization. And those mid-twentieth-century critiques inevitably return to the previous century and to slavery and its many perversions of justice. In words remembered as spoken by the father of fictional black detective Toussaint Marcus Moore, hero of Ed Lacy's (nom de plume of Leonard S. Zinberg) political pulp novel, *Room to Swing*, as he is facing "a white cop and black me": "A Negro's life is dirt cheap because he hasn't any rights a white man must respect. That's the law, the Dred Scott Decision, son" (69). So the debates about black consciousness and state violence against the black body extended beyond philosophy and politics, spreading into popular culture as well during the 1950s.

Fanon's critique of Sartre's dialectical (mis)understanding of blackness at the abyss contemplated in his preface to a collection of poetry sends us back to Césaire's *Notebook of a Return to My Native Land* to think again about Fanon's desire for "black impulsiveness," for a refusal of the simplistic Marxist equation of races with classes, for the denatured recourse to historical necessity and "the circumstances of history," as Sartre calls them, that superintend poetry and futurity: Césaire, as noted by Sartre and then quoted by Fanon, calls out to "raise the great Negro shout with a force that will shake the foundations of the world" (113). So it is voice, the shout, but perhaps more to the point merely the three words gasped in a whisper before unconsciousness and death, that echo throughout and beyond Fanon's text.

As Fanon wryly remarks, "Expressing the real is an arduous job" (116). He continues, "Jean-Paul Sartre forgets that the black man suffers in his body quite differently from the white man" (117). Fanon stresses again and again that black expression is embodied—the shout emanates from within black corporeality, one that is on false display in Paris in the posters of Senegalese soldiers: "The grinning *Y a bon Banania*" (92). Fanon's turn to popular culture, in the form of advertisements and billboards, demonstrates a pervasive and casual expression of the "real" of white violence and its effects on everyday black life. Ultimately invoking Richard Wright's 1941 phototextual documentary, *12 Million Black Voices* (which he names in English), Fanon argues for countering white racist violence "tactually and affectively" through body and voice (67): "The former slave wants his humanity to be challenged; he is looking for a fight; he wants a brawl. . . . In the United States the black man fights and is fought against. . . . *The twelve million black voices* have screamed against the curtain of the sky. And the curtain, torn from end to end, gashed by the teeth biting its belly of prohibitions, has fallen" (196). Mouth, teeth, even fists resist. Beyond Césaire and the other poets invoked, Fanon sends us to Wright's 1940 novel *Native Son* and his documentary phototextual book published the following year—and thus to the United States (Chester Himes is also present, so he's referencing the black expatriates hanging out at the Café Tournon in Paris; thus America is attenuated for African-American writers living abroad). These works and their writers are not only living as nonnative sons but come out of black writers' encounters with the Communist Party of the United States of America (CPUSA) and its organizations, including the Civil Rights Congress, which a few years later in 1951, the year before Fanon published *Black Skin, White Masks*, would submit the petition *We Charge Genocide: The Historic Petition to the United Nations for Relief from a Crime of the United States Government against the Negro People*—but that's another story, an American story barely edging Fanon's work, though front and center for the United States today.

The twelve million black voices actually cannot be heard—at least not at first. Instead, Wright reveals them through what can be seen—or, more accurately, what cannot be seen—because black time and space follow maps virtually uncharted:

> Each day when you see us black folk upon the dusty land or the farms or upon the hard pavement of the city streets, you usually take us for granted and think you know us, but our history is far stranger than you suspect, and we are not what we seem. Our outward guise still carries the old familiar aspect which three hundred years of oppression in America have given us, but beneath the garb of the black laborer, the black cook, and black elevator operator lies an uneasily tied knot of pain and hope whose snarled strands converge from many points of time and space. (10–11)

In his invocation of an "outward guise" conveyed in various places and covering over a strange history (thus, a black chronotope), Wright himself is returning to his source—W. E. B. Du Bois, of course—who comments in "The Forethought" to *The Souls of Black Folk* (1903) on the spatiotemporality of American racial discourse, "the strange meaning of being black here at the dawning of the Twentieth Century," one, in his famous words, of a "two-ness," which resulted, in his corpsed view, that "he saw himself,—darkly as through a veil" (v).[3]

The two-ness Du Bois first limned in "Strivings of the Negro People," published in 1897—"an American, a Negro; two souls, two thoughts, two unreconciled strivings; two warring ideals in one dark body, whose dogged strength alone keeps it from being torn asunder" (194)—also collapses time and space within black subjectivity. The brawl Fanon imagines tearing the curtain of the sky and the teeth gnashing racism's belly are not only public expressions conveyed through mass uprising but are also warring within the black body, a warring black body under siege within the warring state it inhabits. But more than body (fists and teeth), or rather deeper within it, gapes "the black abyss of language" Marriott discerns from Césaire: voices (from Wright); souls (from Du Bois). These immaterials, there without physicality but nevertheless producing deadly effect, must combat (using his word) the "*inhumanising*" and "unreadable rupture or fissure" of racism—the insidious racism and its attendant cowardly shame that even infects Césaire when he encountered the "COMICAL AND UGLY" black man on the tram and "sported a great smile of complicity" (69). And thus, in David Marriott's words, he must recognize that "for black self-liberation to take place, the equation of language with humanity is in question."

Through Césaire, Fanon, and Sartre, Marriott asks us to listen to the sounds of a dying colonialism, then conceptualize and articulate a response to the words of the soon-to-be corpses and the corpsing of those who have been exposed for all to see by Black Lives Matter and the ongoing political agitation against police brutality in the black community. To do this, we must inhabit differently, as we all do every day everywhere, the dark veil, the violence of racism. We must see it, see through it; for some, for the first time; for others, sadly, perpetually. Fanon declares he "endeavored to sense from the inside the despair of the black man confronted with the white man . . . attempted to touch on the misery of the black man—tactually and affectively" (67). He goes on, eschewing any claims to objectivity, "I did not want to be objective. Besides, that would have been dishonest: I found it impossible to be objective" (67). Fanon, like his mentor, Césaire, insists on remaking language and consciousness, through language—an in-spiration, a practice thoroughly embodied, like breathing or touching (at once physical and emotional—tactual and affective). David Marriott explores how this might be achieved, how self-alienation must be recognized even as it cannot be named—language too dead, too corpsed, for this to happen, especially in the face of sustained racism—but still essential. For what else is there? This dead and murderous language, our language, propels "the real leap." The matter of black lives is lived within the screams and whispers of abased language and deadly violence; so perhaps it is poetry—the form that makes language strange and makes us see behind the veil into a history far stranger (and does so through voice)—that can best express the real of how precariously, how preciously, black lives matter.

This was the substance of the poem, from the 1895 volume *Majors and Minors* by Paul Laurence Dunbar, that likely provided Du Bois his profound metaphor. "We Wear the Mask" asks us to consider black skin and white masks in a doubly dialectical and subversive way: a way of reading that makes vivid the strangeness of matter—the very state of things, seen and unseen, things as they are and as they come into visibility, paradoxically by masking—as a continuous interruptive performance. A performance recognized by those cognizant of the stakes yet utterly missed by most. So I conclude by taking us back even further to resuscitate another early instance of black poesis, to the moment of *Plessy v. Ferguson* and its codification of Jim Crow that refigured the original sin, the one never redeemed, of slavery.[4] Donning the mask of the sonnet, Dunbar revealed what was the matter:

> We wear the mask that grins and lies,
> It hides our cheeks and shades our eyes,—
> This debt we pay to human guile;
> With torn and bleeding hearts we smile
> And mouth with myriad subtleties,
>
> Why should the world be over-wise,
> In counting all our tears and sighs?
> Nay, let them only see us, while
> We wear the mask.
>
> We smile, but oh great Christ, our cries
> To thee from tortured souls arise.
> We sing, but oh the clay is vile
> Beneath our feet, and long the mile,
> But let the world dream otherwise,
> We wear the mask! (21)

Masking, corpsing. These are theatrical moves, performances requiring both veiling and visibility done on the sly, yet signaling their appearance. It is in this contradictory frame that the matter of black life must be expressed, felt, and defended.

Paula Rabinowitz is professor emerita of English at the University of Minnesota. Her recent books include *American Pulp: How Paperbacks Brought Modernism to Main Street* (2014) and the four-volume coedited series *Habits of Being* (Minnesota, 2011–15). She is editor-in-chief of the *Oxford Research Encyclopedia of Literature*.

Notes

1. I also want to thank the organizers of the symposium "The State of Things": John Mowitt, Simona Sawhney, and Cesare Casarino—as well as Tom Cannavino, for giving me the opportunity to comment on David Marriott's brilliant work. I came to the University of Minnesota in 1987—hired by John Mowitt to teach American women's and minority literatures and feminist and film theories—in part because of the University of Minnesota Press's Theory and History of Literature series and *Cultural Critique*. These publications disseminated the work we wanted to read as graduate students and these were the venues where we hoped to be published. And in my final year as a professor here, I can say—I succeeded! However, the University of Minnesota has been and continues to be among the least racially diverse campuses within major research institutions, with a long-standing history of failure to recruit and retain faculty and students of color, an issue being challenged once again by students through their organizing the Whose Diversity? actions.

2. I thank him as well for introducing the term to me and my husband, who has spent decades in theater and never encountered it (a Britishism reminiscent of but different from either an actor's despair ["I'm dying out here"] or exaltation ["I'm killing them"]), though he certainly had experienced the situation.

3. From "Of the Training of Black Men":

From the shimmering swirl of waters where many, many thoughts ago the slave-ship first saw the square tower of Jamestown, have flowed down to our day three streams of thinking: one swollen from the larger world here and overseas, saying, the multiplying of human wants in culture-lands calls for the world-wide cooperation of men in satisfying them. Hence arises a new human unity, pulling the ends of earth nearer, and all men, black, yellow, and white. The larger humanity strives to feel in this contact of living Nations and sleeping hordes a thrill of new life in the world, crying, "If the contact of Life and Sleep be Death, shame on such Life." To be sure, behind this thought lurks the afterthought of force and dominion,—the making of brown men to delve when the temptation of beads and red calico cloys.

The second thought streaming from the death-ship and the curving river is the thought of the older South,—the sincere and passionate belief that somewhere between men and cattle, God created a *tertium quid*, and called it a Negro,—a clownish, simple creature, at times even lovable within its limitations, but straitly foreordained to walk within the Veil. To be sure, behind the thought lurks the afterthought,—some of them with favoring chance might become men, but in sheer self-defence we dare not let them, and we build about them walls so high, and hang between them and the light a veil so thick, that they shall not even think of breaking through.

And last of all there trickles down that third and darker thought,— the thought of the things themselves, the confused, half-conscious mutter of men who are black and whitened, crying "Liberty, Freedom, Opportunity—vouchsafe to us, O boastful World, the chance of living men!" To be sure, behind the thought lurks the afterthought,—suppose, after all, the World is right and we are less than men? Suppose this mad impulse within is all wrong, some mock mirage from the untrue? (55–56)

4. See Lipsitz in a special section, "In the Conjuncture," of *Cultural Critique*, "For Michael Brown," for more on the link between Gilded Age Jim Crow and our current moment of racial violence and radical inequality.

Works Cited

Ao, Temsula. 2006. *These Hills Called Home: Stories from a War Zone*. New Delhi: Zubaan, Kali for Women.

Césaire, Aimé. 1969. *Return to My Native Land*. Trans. John Berger and Anna Bostock. Harmondsworth: Penguin Books. (Orig. pub. 1939.)

Civil Rights Congress. 1951. *We Charge Genocide: The Historic Petition to the United Nations for Relief from a Crime of the United States Government against the Negro People*. New York: Civil Rights Congress.

Du Bois, W. E. B. 1897. "Strivings of the Negro People." *Atlantic Monthly* (August): 194–97.

———. 1994. *The Souls of Black Folk*. New York: Dover. (Orig. pub. 1903.)

Dunbar, Paul Laurence. 1895. "We Wear the Mask." In *Majors and Minors: Poems*, 21. Toledo, Ohio: Hadley and Hadley.

Fanon, Frantz. 2008. *Black Skin, White Masks*. Trans. Richard Philcox. New York: Grove Press. (Orig. pub. 1952.)

Hurston, Zora Neale. 2015. *How It Feels to Be Colored Me*. Carlisle, Mass.: Applewood Books. (Orig. pub. 1928.)

Lacy, Ed [Leonard S. Zinberg]. 1957. *Room to Swing*. New York: Pyramid Books.

Lipsitz, George. 2015. "From *Plessy* to Ferguson." *Cultural Critique* 90 (Spring): 119–39.

Marriott, David. 2016. "Corpsing; or, The Matter of Black Life." *Cultural Critique* 94 (Fall): 32–64.

McBride, Eimear. 2013. *A Girl Is a Half-Formed Thing*. Norwich: Galley Beggar Press.

Patterson, Orlando. 1982. *Slavery and Social Death: A Comparative Study.* Cambridge, Mass.: Harvard University Press.

Rose, Jacqueline. 2016. "Feminism and the Abomination of Violence." *Cultural Critique* 94 (Fall): 4–25.

Schmidt, Michael S., and Matt Apuzzo. 2015. "White House Disagrees with F.B.I. Chief on Scrutiny as a Cause of Crime." *New York Times*, October 27.

Wright, Richard. 2002. *12 Million Black Voices.* New York: Thunder's Mouth Press. (Orig. pub. 1941.)

A VIEW FROM THE SIDE
THE NATURAL HISTORY MUSEUM

Jodi Dean

THE ANAMORPHIC POLITICS OF CLIMATE CHANGE

The challenge of politics in the Anthropocene is a matter of perspective: we can't look at climate change directly. We look for patterns and estimate probabilities, relying on multiple disparate measurements. We see in parts: the melting ice caps, glaciers, and permafrost; the advancing deserts and diminishing coral reefs; the disappearing coastlines and the migrating species. Evidence becomes a matter of extremes as extremes themselves become evidence of an encroaching catastrophe that has already happened: the highest recorded temperatures, the hockey stick of predicted warming, sea-level rise, and extinction. Once we see it—the "it" of climate change encapsulated into a data point or disastrous image—it's too late. For what and for whom remains unsaid, unknowable.[1]

Climate change tethers us to a perspective that oscillates between the impossible and the inevitable, already and not yet, everywhere but not here, not quite. Slavoj Žižek reminds us that such oscillation indexes the "too much or too little" of enjoyment *(jouissance)*. For psychoanalysis, particularly in Lacan's teaching, enjoyment is a special substance, that intense pleasure/pain that makes life worth living and some things worth dying for. We will do *anything* to get what we think we will enjoy. We then discover after we get it that it wasn't what we *really* desired after all. Enjoyment is what we want but can't get and what we get that we don't want.[2]

Currents of Left anthropocenic enjoyment circulate via evocations of unprecedented, unthinkable catastrophe: the end of the world, the end of the human species, the end of civilization.[3] Prophetic Cassandras condemn all around them for our profligacy, even as they imply that there isn't anything we can do. The damage has already been done.

The perfect storm of planetary catastrophe, species condemnation, and paralyzed incapacity lets the Left enjoy in ways that ongoing deprivation, responsibility, and struggle do not. Left anthropocenic enjoyment thereby feeds on the disaster capitalist enjoyment produces. More, more, more; endless circulation, dispossession, destruction, and accumulation; ceaseless, limitless death. Incapacitated by magnitude, boggled by scale, the Left gets off on moralism, complexity, and disaster—even as politics continues, the politics of a capitalist class determined to profit from catastrophe.

If fascination with climate change's anthropocenic knot of catastrophe, condemnation, and paralysis lures the Left into the loop of capitalist enjoyment, an anamorphic gaze can help dislodge us. "Anamorphosis" designates an image or object that seems distorted when we look at it head on but that appears clearly from another perspective. Jacques Lacan (1998) emphasizes that anamorphosis demonstrates how the space of vision isn't reducible to mapped space. It includes the point from which we see. Space can be distorted, depending on how we look at it. Apprehending what is significant, then, may require "escaping the fascination of the picture" by adopting another perspective, a partial or partisan perspective, the perspective of a part. From a partisan perspective, the whole will not appear as a whole. It will appear with a hole. The perspective from which the hole appears is that of the subject— that is, of the gap that the shift to a partisan perspective opens up.

When we try to grasp climate change directly, we trap ourselves in distortions that fuel the reciprocal fantasies of planetary-scale geoengineering and postcivilizational neoprimitivism. The immensity of the calamity of the changing climate—with attendant desertification, ocean acidification, and species loss—seemingly forces us into seeing all or nothing. If we don't grasp the issue in its enormity, we miss it entirely. When we approach climate change indirectly, from the side, however, other openings, political openings, become visible. Rather than being ensnared by our fascination with an illusory anthropocenic whole, we cut across and through, gaining possibilities for collective action and strategic engagement.

Here are some examples of approaching climate change from the side. Christian Parenti (2011) emphasizes the "catastrophic convergence" of poverty, violence, and climate change. He draws out the uneven and unequal impacts of planetary warming on areas already devastated by capitalism, racism, colonialism, and militarism. From this angle, policies aimed at redressing and reducing economic inequality appear as necessary adaptations to a changing climate. In a similar vein, but on a different scale, activists focused on pipeline and oil and gas storage projects target the fossil fuel industry as the infrastructure of climate change, the central component of warming's means of reproduction. Instead of exemplifying a tired politics of locality, infrastructure struggles pursue the anamorphic politics of climate change. They don't try to address the whole of the causes and effects of global warming. They approach it from the side, the side of its infrastructural supports.

The NHM, the new project of the art, activist, and theory collective Not An Alternative, likewise pursues an anamorphic politics. In this ongoing performance, Not An Alternative adopts the legitimating aesthetics, pedagogical models, and presentation forms of natural history museums in support of a divisive perspective on science, nature, and capitalism. With the NHM, Not An Alternative does not try to present climate change directly or nature as a whole. Instead, the project approaches our setting from the side, through examinations of labor history, social movements, public relations, and practices of science

Figure 1. The Natural History Museum, workshop, 2014. NHM workshops train participants to take the view of museum anthropologists who are attuned to the social and political forces shaping nature. Photograph by the NHM.

communication. The NHM puts displays on display, transferring our attention to the infrastructures supporting what and how we see. Its anamorphic gaze is avowedly partisan, a political approach to climate change in the context of a museum culture that revels in its "authoritative neutrality." The NHM activates the natural history museum's claim to serve the common, thereby dividing the museum from within: anyone connected to the museum sector, anyone tasked with communicating science and natural history to a wider public, has to take a side. Do they stand with collectivity and the common or with oligarchs, private property, and the fossil fuel industry?

This essay focuses on the innovative artistic and political practice evinced by the NHM. I situate the project in Not An Alternative's work as politically engaged artists, attending to some of the ways the NHM responds to problems that arise in the overlap of socially engaged art and institutional critique, understanding this response as lessons for politics in the Anthropocene.[4] The NHM is, first, a platform for political organizing that treats the museum, science, and nature as sites of struggle. As a platform, the NHM moves beyond socially engaged art's creation of experiences and valuation of participation for its own sake to function as an organizing tool for building divisive political power. The NHM, second, is an artistic project that confiscates the form of the natural history museum in order to direct us toward what the museum as an institution excludes—namely, the place of power and politics in determining how we see and what is possible. Extending institutional critique (work from artists such as Hans Haacke, Fred Wilson, Mark Dion, and Andrea Fraser), the NHM locates the limits to a system within the system. The repercussion is that working within a system becomes not cooptation and complicity but occupation and seizure. Consequently, third, the NHM is a theoretical laboratory for experiments in seizing the state by seizing the institutions that transmit knowledge and legitimacy—experiments, in other words, in the building of a counterpower infrastructure. The wide array of operations that constitute the project demonstrate a capacity for political organization and strategy, one the can be adopted, amplified, and extended. In fact, Not An Alternative's NHM is a project that shares with other recent projects an emphasis on the politics of the institution: for example, Jonas Staal's New World Summit and Liberate Tate's efforts to liberate cultural institutions from the oil industry, specifically BP. In contrast with Left anthropocenic enjoyment of failure, moralism, and catastrophe, lessons in institutionality hold open the promise of and need for collective struggle.

Too many contemporary discussions of the Anthropocene so obscure the organization of people—our institutions, systems, and arrangements of power, production, and reproduction—that they appear only as distortions. Everything is active except for us. In contrast with emphases on nonhumans, actants, and vibrant matter, I am interested in the political subject as it registers in the gap between the haste of an action and the retroactive determination of this precipitous act as the act of a collective political subject.[5] We shouldn't undermine collective political power in the name of a moralistic horizontalism of humans and nonhumans. We should work to generate collective power and mobilize it in an emancipatory egalitarian direction, a direction incompatible with the continuation of capitalism and hence a direction necessarily partisan and divisive. The NHM, along with other projects of institutional liberation, pushes the imagining, production, and organization of such a power in the context of the resource struggles of the Anthropocene. Through their work, the people appear with a capacity to effect political change.

Figure 2. Not An Alternative demonstration and attempted occupation of a park following the eviction of the Occupy Wall Street encampment, 2011. Photograph by Not An Alternative.

Figure 3. Not An Alternative candlelight vigil following the eviction of the Occupy Wall Street encampment, 2011. Photograph by Not An Alternative.

Figure 4. Not An Alternative, Occupy Town Square, and Pratt Disaster Resilience Network directing residents impacted by Superstorm Sandy to relief stations administered by Occupy organizers. Photograph by Not An Alternative.

INSTITUTIONALITY, AT A MINIMUM

As is clear from its name, Not An Alternative twists Margaret Thatcher's infamous "there is no alternative" to shift from something in the negative to nothing in the positive. This "nothing" is an interior antagonism, an object's nonidentity with itself, the inherent limit of a system, or the gap constitutive of the subject. Not An Alternative's projects aim to find and occupy the impossible instances of a given system, splitting the system by forcing its internal limits back onto it and seizing the common, egalitarian potential that is already present.[6] Forcing of a lack opens the space of the subject; seizing the common demonstrates fidelity to the people as that subject.

Not An Alternative developed its position in part via a critique of communicative capitalism—more specifically, via a critique of the injunction to participate that infuses the contemporary intertwining of democracy and capitalism. In a context where activists and artists were repeating communicative capitalism's demand for participation as if participation were in and of itself a radical or emancipatory act, Not An Alternative emphasized how networked media involves us in building the traps that ensnare us. The group explains, "We come up with new forms and they are integrated directly as fuel for a system that is fundamentally unsustainable. Our solutions are sucked into the brand identities of institutions. As Not An Alternative, we are not interested in the production of solutions or the inclusion of new subjectivities or symbols, but rather the excavation and occupation of existing ones, revealing an inherent split" (Donovan). Under conditions of the proliferation of memes and images, of capitalist efforts to identify and monetize whatever is new and different and intense competition for positions, recognition, and capital, producing the new feeds the system. In the name of democratic participation, artists and activists end up reinforcing dominant processes of multiplication and diffusion.[7] Treating democracy as the value to be realized, they proceed as if politics were nothing more than social engagement. The role of the artist then becomes creating new openings through which people might engage and be engaged. Not An Alternative breaks with socially engaged art in that it views politics antagonistically. Political art should occupy division and force the institution to take a side.

Not An Alternative's work takes the form of installations, interventions in arts institutions and public spaces, and political collaborations. Collaborations have been with community groups (for example, Occupy Sandy and Picture the Homeless, a housing advocacy group in NYC), activist campaigns (Strike Debt), and social movements (Occupy Wall Street, antiforeclosure, climate justice). In these collaborations, Not An Alternative has two aims: to find the limits of a given system and to assemble a symbolic infrastructure that links groups and actions, making disparate actions and campaigns legible as fronts in one struggle. So even as Not An Alternative's work stretches from video and performance, through museums and urban spaces, to research and organizing, it is marked by what Yates McKee (2013) calls a "militant uniformity." This militant uniformity comes from the common, the visual systems that continue to signify some minimal degree of institutionality in our setting of the decline of symbolic efficiency.

Not An Alternative came up with Occupy's black-and-yellow symbolic infrastructure (McKee 2014). This infrastructure takes the color scheme and style associated with public works such as construction sites and highway caution signage and puts it in the hands of the people. With this visual infrastructure, Not An Alternative presented the occupation in terms of what was common: common tactics carried out under a name in common. Rather than a marker left by capitalism and the state, the signage points to the common interest of the people, to the division they share in common. When activists reappropriate warning tape and caution signage, they force the question: in whose interest is power exercised? During Occupy, the "militant uniformity" of the yellow and black helped make a collective subject present to itself, enabling it to feel itself as a collective force.

Likewise, in contrast with the familiar critique of representation, Not An Alternative demonstrated the power of representation.[8] It pulled out a visual element of the movement—tents—forcing acknowledgement of the way tents already functioned as clear symbols of occupation. Where various activist, artistic, and theoretical voices reject representation for its inevitable omissions, a rejection anchored in the fantasy of a pure, complete, and direct representation, a fantasy of absolute and unmediated inclusion, Not An Alternative recognizes that representations attempt to produce their subjects (Steyerl, 17).[9] A shared image or point of identification, a name in common, affects those who identify it as a marker of collectivity—whether they identify with it as their own or see it as designating an enemy. Because of Occupy, tents assumed a political meaning that had remained implicit in their range of appearings in refugee camps and the temporary encampments that sprung up outside U.S. cities in the economic downturn. People were asserting themselves in places where they did not belong, refusing to accept any longer the barriers posed by capital and the state. Whether or not every occupier was actually living in a tent, tents signified occupation, pressing the divisive claim of the people against the one percent. Not An Alternative's "mili-tents," carried in actions and attached to walls even after police had cleared all the occupiers out of Zuccotti Park, both pointed to the fundamental division in capitalism that Occupy asserted and highlighted the symbolic infrastructure the movement itself was producing.

Not An Alternative's practice is situated in the overlap between socially engaged art and "institutional critique." Initially appearing at the end of the 1960s, institutional critique has gone through two and arguably even three waves.[10] Given current discussion of these waves, it is perhaps most accurate to locate Not An Alternative's practice in the critique of institutional critique that emerged in the second and third waves in the 1990's and 2000's; to locate it, in other words, in institutional critique's own self-reflection.

The first wave of institutional critique developed an immanent critique of the institution of art, applying to museums normative criteria that the museums themselves claimed to hold. Crucial to this critique was the exposure not simply of the market dimension of art but of the role of class in determining what counts as art and the role of art in establishing the signifiers of class.[11] Artists such as Hans Haacke, a key influence on Not An Alternative, extended the idea of the "institution" beyond spaces for the teaching, viewing, production, and selling of art to encompass "the network of social and economic relationships between them" (Fraser, 412).

The second wave of institutional critique focused on the limits of institutional critique. Did institutional critique's dependence on the institution it was critiquing in some way compromise it, making it just as guilty and complicit as the gallery or museum? Did attempts to find loci of independence backfire when an institution happily sponsored "external" critical perspectives as aesthetic events from which the institution itself was critically shielded or immunized, its political credentials established by the fact of its sponsorship? As Fraser argues in her influential 2006 essay, "It is artists—as much as museums or the market—who, in their very efforts to escape the institution of art, have driven its expansion. With each attempt to evade the limits of institutional determination, to embrace an outside, to redefine art or reintegrate it into everyday life, to reach 'everyday' people and work in the 'real' world, we expand our frame and bring more of the world into it. But we never escape it" (414). Inclusion in the institution serves as the very means by which political effects are precluded, deactivated. Expanding the frame spreads political deactivation. Once everything is art, included within and supporting the institutional frame, nothing is political.

Not An Alternative accepts Fraser's point that escape is impossible—there is no outside. With Lacanian theory as an explicit part of its practice, Not An Alternative locates the limit within the institution.[12] No institution is fully self-identical. Institutions are split between the ideals they espouse and their actual practices, between the practices they openly acknowledge and the obscene rituals they have to deny. Not An Alternative thus turns the institution against itself, siding with its better nature, and forcing others to take a side. It looks for allies, "double agents" already working within the institution, reinforces them, and in so doing activates the power that is already there. So rather than just making complicity with state and capital visible, Not An Alternative treats institutions as forms to be seized and connected into a counterpower infrastructure. Fraser writes, "It's not a question of being against the institution: We are the institution. It's a question of what kind of institution we are, what kind of values we institutionalize, what forms of practice we reward, and what kinds of rewards we aspire to" (416). Emphasizing the "we," Fraser points to the necessity of a partisan position. Not just any values, and certainly not all values, are politically compatible with the institution "we" are. The institution is the site of a larger struggle, a territory or apparatus that can be commandeered.

This is the overlap between Not An Alternative's critique of participation and its institutional critique. In each case it emphasizes the importance of division, taking a side. Not An Alternative rejects the supposition of some socially engaged art that the goal is creative experience and inclusive participation. Instead, it embraces militant opposition, tight organizational forms, and the aggregated power of institutions. It insists as well on the struggle that continues within any group, form, or institution. Division goes all the way down. Self-identity is a fantasy. Not An Alternative further rejects both the melancholic claims of contemporary depoliticization and a politics thought in terms of resistance, insurrection, playful aesthetic disruptions, and the establishment of momentary relations of community and belonging. It aims to occupy institutions, build counterpower infrastructure, and develop strategies. Not An Alternative rejects familiar calls for innovation. Instead, it salvages the generic images, practices, institutions, and forms that have already compiled and stored collective power. Here it claims the continued power of communism as the name for an anticapitalism oriented toward the collective desire for collectivity.

To sum up, for Not An Alternative, institutions are sites of collective power. It models a Leninist strategy for seizing the state under conditions of communicative capitalism as it takes over available signifying modes and reclaims the communicative common of language, ideas, knowledge, and affects. This is a politics of organization, infrastructure, and counterpower. To the extent that Not An Alternative's projects do not simply create momentary social relations or open participatory social spaces but actually build a partisan counterpower infrastructure, their work moves beyond socially engaged art to the art of political engagement; an art that, no longer confined with the suppositions of a democratic imaginary, takes communism as its horizon.

BEING THE MUSEUM

Not An Alternative's current multiyear project, the NHM, employs the visual and communicative practices of natural history museums to perform a sort of "people's natural history"—that is to say, a natural history that includes the struggles of the oppressed and laboring classes. Instead of relying on aesthetic gestures of critique, irony, or the retreat into poetic reverie found in some ecological art, Not An Alternative takes on the generic form of the natural history museum. Becoming the institution allows it to incorporate sincerity, commitment, partisanship, and truth into a politically engaged artwork. The NHM isn't a joke or

Figure 5. The NHM, workshop, 2014. NHM workshops train participants to take the view of museum anthropologists who are attuned to the social and political forces shaping nature. Photograph by the NHM.

a stunt. It's a registered member of the American Alliance of Museums. It has a board that includes prominent scientists (James Powell), artists (Mark Dion), and environmental activists (Naomi Klein). It doesn't exist as a building. It exists as an insistent collective perspective on the common.

As an artistic project, the NHM installs a gap between the expectations associated with the natural history museum form and its own displays. These include re-creations of dioramas from other natural history museums as well as letters, petitions, campaigns, articles, and events authorized by the museum. By exhibiting how nature appears, the NHM opens up not only the irreducibility of nature to its appearing but also the gap of human systems, perceptions, and institutions within nature. This gap forces "visitors" (whether construed as the specific museum professionals addressed in some exhibitions and organizing efforts or more broadly as anyone who comes in contact with the name "Natural History Museum") to acknowledge the place from which they see.

The museum as an institution works allegorically as a screen through which to access the real of political antagonism occluded in the moralizing and technocratic discourses of the Anthropocene. A natural history museum is a collective perspective on a common world. Visitors to the NHM encounter themselves *as a collective* in their act of looking: how does the common appear in this institution dedicated to fostering appreciation of the natural world, and how is what is common excluded? With this reflexive torsion, the NHM holds open the gap it installs, politicizing it as a collective desire for collectivity.

The NHM functions as a campaign and counterinstitution. As a political campaign, it challenges fossil fuel industry greenwashing in natural history museums. Here it provides a platform for calls for fossil fuel divestment. The NHM's specific targets are the cultural institutions that communicate knowledge of science and nature: museums that retain a great deal of public trust but which provide legitimating opportunities for coal, oil, and gas companies. Fossil fuel oligarchs like David R. Koch sit on the boards of and are major donors to such influential museums as the American Museum of Natural History in New York and the Smithsonian Institute in Washington, D.C. The dinosaur wing in the American Museum of Natural History, for example, is named after Koch, who donated twenty million dollars to the museum. To combat this oligarchic influence, the NHM organizes scientists, museum workers, and museum visitors to stand with and for the common over and against capitalist extraction, exploitation, and expropriation.

Although it does not have a permanent brick-and-mortar (or steel-and-glass) base, the NHM does have a bus. It uses the bus for expeditions to sites such as Sunset Park, Brooklyn, an area within New York

Figure 6. The NHM, Kick Koch off the Board, 2015. The NHM joined forces with 150 of the world's top scientists, including several Nobel laureates, and more than 550,000 members of the public to urge New York's American Museum of Natural History to kick climate denier David Koch off its board. After 23 years on the board, Koch resigned amid controversy in December 2015. Graphic by the NHM.

Figure 7. The NHM exhibition poster, 2014. The NHM's inaugural exhibition took place at Queens Museum in 2014. It featured photography, taxidermic specimens, and programming with scientists, artists, historians, anthropologists, media theorists, and climate justice activists. Graphic by the NHM.

City's storm surge zone; eleven oil wells in the Big Cypress National Reserve in the Florida swampland; and Washington, D.C., for the delivery of a petition with over four hundred thousand signatories demanding that the Smithsonian Institute remove Koch from its board.[13] Reports of the NHM's expeditions appear regularly on its website.

Launched to coincide with the People's Climate March, the NHM opened in September 2014 with an exhibition and discussion series in the New York City building at the Queens Museum. The NHM's opening exhibition was set inside a sixty-four-foot tent inside the building. It featured a series of light boxes with photographs of dioramas from various natural history museums. The diorama is the aesthetic form most associated with the twentieth-century natural history museum. It doesn't attempt to impart information so much as it tries to convey feelings of wonder. Its romantic, idealized, and hyperrealistic displays bring the aura of nature into the museum. The NHM's light boxes showed this display. Some of the photographs included the people looking at the dioramas. Others seemed to emanate from within the dioramas. The NHM's opening also included a two-month discussion series. Taking place inside the tent, the series included artists, writers, and activists organized into panels on institutional critique, the Anthropocene, museum patronage, urban planning, and climate justice.

Figure 8. The NHM, Citizen Science Expedition, 2014. The NHM's fifteen-passenger mobile museum bus is used to transport scientists, artists, activists, and members of the public on tours and field expeditions. Photograph by the NHM.

The enormous tent gave the feeling of both an exhibition and an expedition. It resonated with Occupy, linking the occupation of the Queens Museum to the political movement and making the natural history museum legible as a political form for climate change struggle. There are natural history museums all over the world, a preexisting infrastructure ready to be activated against those who would use it to legitimate continued drilling, fracking, and coal, oil, and gas production. In the position of political collectivity, the tent amplifies the affective engagement that accompanies the "diorama feeling" of nature's power and vulnerability, otherness and awe. Under the same tent, visitors become part of the collective that is splitting the museum between the people and the corporation, oligarchy, or industry seeking to present knowledge in its interest. The NHM's tent turns visitors into occupiers, implicating them in a counterpower infrastructure. It divides the space of its installation within itself, creating a new, divisive collectivity.

As I mentioned, the NHM is a dues-paying member of the American Alliance of Museums (AAM). Less than six months after the NHM's launch, its director was invited to serve as a guest author of the blog of the AAM's key initiatives.[14] At the MuseumExpo accompanying the AAM's 2015 annual meeting, the NHM had the largest exhibition space. It brought its bus and enormous tent into the Georgia World Congress Center in Atlanta, where it highlighted fossil fuel industry greenwashing in science and natural history museums. Volunteers from the NHM distributed fliers to visitors with answers to questions commonly posed to museum professionals trying to navigate through the funding pressures of neoliberal capitalism and the ideology of "authoritative neutrality" in the context of climate change.

One large installation re-created the famous polar bear diorama from New York's American Museum of Natural History's 2009 climate change exhibition. The NHM's version included previously excluded political–economic content regarding David Koch, who at the time served as a member of the board of the American Museum of Natural History. Where the original diorama featured a polar bear confronting the detritus of consumerism, the NHM's diorama exposed what lies beneath the surface: a large oil pipe from Koch Industries. The NHM pushes to the surface the infrastructure that the American Museum of Natural History would prefer to keep submerged: the fossil fuel

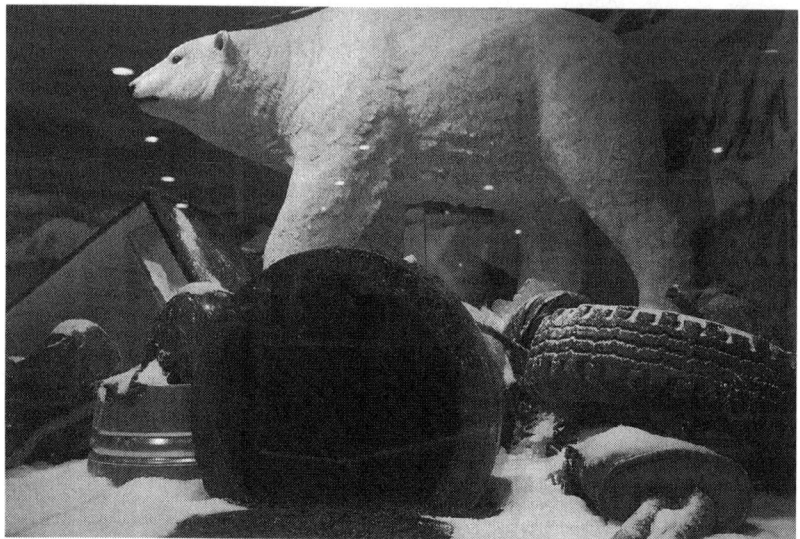

Figure 9. The NHM, *Our Climate, Whose Politics?*, 2015. Diorama in an exhibition at the American Alliance of Museums Annual Convention, Atlanta, Ga., depicting a diorama from a climate change exhibition at New York's American Museum of Natural History with the inclusion of a Koch Industries pipeline. Photograph by the NHM.

industry driving climate change that also supports the American Museum of Natural History.

A second installation gestured to Hans Haacke's 2014 show at the Paula Cooper Gallery. Haacke not only exhibited a number of water pieces but also showed a new work attacking the Metropolitan Museum of Art for its new David H. Koch Plaza. This work displayed fake hundred dollar bills flowing down out of images of the new Koch fountain. The NHM installation continued the deployment of fountains, water, tubing, and Koch's use of the cultural capital of museums to deflect critique from his consistent use of the political system to thwart environmental regulations. The installation featured a water system comprised of two tanks and a water fountain. One tank was identified as water from the American Museum of Natural History. Its accompanying description, modeled after a similar description used at the American Museum of Natural History, commends the cleanliness of New York City water. The second tank of water is identified as coming from North Pole, Alaska. This water is contaminated by sulfolane, a chemical from a Koch-owned refinery that leaked for years into the community's groundwater, making it undrinkable. The NHM's water system displays the pipes and tubes connecting the tanks and the fountain (itself a direct replica of one in the American Museum of Natural History).

In March 2015 the NHM released an open letter to museums of science and natural history signed by dozens of the world's top scientists, including several Nobel laureates. The letter urged museums to cut all ties with the fossil fuel industry and with funders of climate obfuscation. After its release, hundreds of scientists added their names. News of the letter went viral, appearing on the front pages of the *New York Times, Washington Post,* and *LA Times,* and featured in the *Guardian, Forbes, Salon, Huffington Post,* and elsewhere. A leading climate change denial and obfuscation organization, the Center for the Study of Carbon Dioxide and Global Change, countered with a petition of its own.[15] One of the signatories is Willie Soon, a solar physicist who works at the Harvard–Smithsonian Center for Astrophysics. Soon attributes climate change to sunspots. He has received over a million dollars in funding from the fossil fuel sector, including the Charles G. Koch Charitable Foundation.[16]

Later in the summer, the NHM's bus operated as a platform for speakers delivering a petition with over four hundred thousand signatories demanding that the Smithsonian Institute remove David Koch from their board. By the end of the summer, it was clear the NHM was having an impact: the California Academy of Sciences, one of the science institutions specifically targeted in a joint initiative of the NHM and 350.org, announced that it was phasing out investments in and relations with the fossil fuel sector. Just a few months later, Koch himself stepped down from his spot on the board of the American Museum of Natural History. Although a spokesperson from the museum said that the campaign against Koch "absolutely did not factor in his decision," all of the coverage of his resignation noted that it was a symbolic victory for the activists.[17]

THE ART OF POLITICAL ENGAGEMENT

Not An Alternative's art of political engagement take shape as four interrelated elements of the NHM: collectivity, division, infrastructure, and truth. Each element is expressed along the three dimensions

I mentioned at the outset: political organizing, artistic project, and theoretical laboratory.

Collectivity

The premise of the NHM as an organizing platform is that institutions matter as combined and intensified expressions of power. More than just the aggregation of individuals, they are individuals plus the force of their aggregation. Because institutions remain concentrations of authority that can be salvaged and put to use, it makes political sense to occupy rather than ignore or abandon them. We can repurpose trusted or taken-for-granted forms.

Natural history and science museums are interesting sites for political seizure and occupation. They retain public confidence as vehicles for science education. At the same time, they are threatened by budget cuts and market imperatives. So they are typically nonprofit, donor- and grant-dependent organizations, focused on cultural rather than commodity production. Yet they are forced to compete for visitors in the dense marketplace of entertainment. This subjects their staffs and boards to a particular pressure: how to retain their commitment to truth and the collective good in the face of opposing political and economic demands. The NHM makes this split within museums explicit. It uses it to organize museum workers, scientists, and visitors. Crucial to this endeavor have been the scientist sign-on letter and the petition calling for museums to break ties with the fossil fuel industry. Aggregated through the NHM, previously disconnected scientists present themselves as a collective force against climate denialism, obfuscation, evasion, and greenwashing. Even more, they *are* a collective force.

The NHM treats its visitors (understood broadly) as split between an understanding that something is wrong with the world and their own position within the world. After thirty years of neoliberalism's intensification of individualism, visitors are likely to relate to the world as individuals and to think of the world's problems as particular (crises, threats, events) rather than as systemic, interconnected. They are unlikely to see themselves as part of a collective that experiences these problems together and as differently—unevenly, unequally—together. Some museum professionals (whether consciously or not) reinforce individualist and individualizing expectations. They conceive exhibitions in terms of individual affective response. They model displays on the basis of individual use of screens and information acquisition. They attend to individual consumption opportunities (souvenirs). In contrast, the NHM presumes an unconscious desire for collectivity. Even if they don't know it, visitors come to the museum looking for connection to a collective and a world from which they feel alienated: in a setting of deep cultural cynicism and mistrust, natural history museums remain among the most trusted institutions.

Expressed in psychoanalytic terms, the consumer orientation of funds-hungry contemporary museums depends on keeping visitors stuck in the circuits of drive, deriving enjoyment from the kicks of catastrophe. It focuses them on spectacles of climate change (extinction, extreme weather) and the ever-receding "great unknown" in nature. In contrast, the NHM incites their desire. Pointing at the capitalist system as the interior limit of what is considered nature, the NHM inscribes a gap in the great unknown. It presents the particular horrors of the world as connected (as systemic). Nature isn't some kind of awesome exterior. It's interior to human economic and political systems.

The NHM, then, operates in one respect as an activist organization, a pop-up museum and alternative institution with a mailing list, social media presence, and menu of cultural offerings. Yet it is also the generic museum that is present in every museum of natural history. It exists to force the already present split toward the common that every particular museum of natural history operating in a capitalist setting is forced to occlude.

Figure 10. The NHM, museum divestment campaign graphic, 2015. The NHM teamed up with the environmental group 350.org to call on top science and natural history museums to divest financial holdings from fossil fuel companies. Graphic by the NHM.

Division

The NHM mobilizes division as it organizes scientists and museum professionals against fossil fuel greenwashing. One of the challenges of this work is the hegemony of the claim that scientists and museums must be neutral, objective, "above" politics. The NHM confronts this claim by pointing out the claim's own limit in the purpose of the museum. As asserted in the Code of Ethics for Museums, the museum is responsible for fostering "an informed appreciation of the rich and diverse world we have inherited" (qtd. in Lyons and Economomopoulos). It is obligated to preserve this inheritance for posterity, providing a common resource for humankind. To this end, natural history museums must not generate legitimacy for those who would undermine the very possibility of a future. The NHM compels the institution to serve the people. Or, better, it enables the institution to function as one of the means through which the people serve themselves—taking care neither to promote the particular interests of billionaires and oligarchs nor to refrain from addressing issues of urgent collective concern.

As the NHM emphasizes in the flier it distributed to museum professionals at the MuseumExpo as well as in an editorial in the *Guardian,* neutrality is a myth. It hides from view the process determining the alternatives toward which it is ostensibly required to be neutral. This process is political. It benefits some and harms others. As Steve Lyons and Beka Economomopoulos (2015) explain, "The claim to authoritative neutrality is dangerous, precisely because it prevents institutions from seriously re-evaluating their roles in a time of climate crisis. At a time when powerful lobbies representing the interests of the fossil fuel industry seek not only to influence public policy but also buy the next election, we can only see neutrality as another word for resignation." In the face of conflict over the truth, the museum loses credibility when it fails to take the side of science. Even worse, it betrays the trust inseparable from its institutional form.

Some view nature in terms of the privilege of the few, the few who can own it, and the few who can access it. Others view nature in terms of all of us, as if we were not divided in our relation to nature, as if nature were not violent, ruptured, cataclysmic. The NHM takes its orientation to nature from two basic insights: nature is common and what is common is divided. We struggle over what is common. We fight to keep it common. The fact of this struggle alerts us to division, conflict, antagonism: nature has never been in balance. Nature doesn't just exist. It insists beyond the limits of the known. What we can't see and don't know impresses itself on how and what we see. The NHM thus brings out the politics excluded from representations of nature as either originally in balance or external to human life. Any demarcation of a field is divisive, an inclusion and an exclusion. The NHM's insistence on division, then, is not in the interest of some fantasy of full inclusion but rather for the purpose of mobilizing the exterior back within the institution. The excluded becomes inflected back in a torsion that repurposes, even reprograms, the institution.

Division goes all the way down. Science is itself divided, a never-ending struggle of methods, metaphors, egos, observations, paradigms, fields, and schools. It proceeds by affirming and rejecting, defending and defeating, knowledge that aspires to truth.

Infrastructure

The NHM seizes and repurposes the generic form of the museum as a set of institutionalized expectations, meanings, and practices that embody and transmit collective power. Cultural institutions tasked with science education become legible in their role in climate change, as sites of greenwashing and counterpower. In this latter sense, the NHM takes hold of the collective that is already present (as institutionality), redirecting it against that which exploits it.[18] Just as the museum is a site in the infrastructure of capitalist class power—with its donors and galas and named halls—so can it be a medium in the production of a counterpower infrastructure that challenges, shames, and dismantles the very class and sector that would use what is common for private benefit.

The aesthetics of the NHM, then, is more than relational. It's political. The intent is not to create a transformational experience or new appreciation of community. It is to achieve concrete political goals: divestment from fossil fuels, organization of scientists into a divisive collective, appropriation of the museum form in climate change struggle, seizure of institutions of knowledge production and cultural transmission, and building a counterpower infrastructure. Here the NHM has more in common with the historic avant-garde than it does with the participatory art of the nineties. As Claire Bishop argues, the former positioned itself in relation to primarily Communist Party politics. The latter hyped itself in communicative capitalist terms that equated participation with democracy even as it lacked both a social and an artistic target (Bishop, 283–84). The NHM doesn't promote awareness and debate. It pushes collective will formation. And it does so by giving a name and form to such a divisive will. As an avant-garde artistic project linked explicitly to an ongoing political movement, the NHM exposes an omission or failure on the contemporary Left: the lack of a revolutionary party or common name and form for the global struggle of the proletarianized.

Truth

The NHM states that its mission is "to affirm the truth of science. By looking at the presentation of natural history, the museum demonstrates principles fundamental to scientific inquiry, principles such as the commonality of knowledge and the unavoidability of the unknown."[19] This mission is a generic statement of the fact that the credibility of museums of natural history comes from their fidelity to truth. Truth is partisan. It's not a matter of consensus. Scientific truth forces itself beyond and through the practices and intentions of those who labor in its name. It is not identical with what scientists do and hence not reducible to its instrumentalization by capitalism and the state. In the theoretical language of Not An Alternative: science is not identical with itself. It is pushed and shaped by the real of a truth exterior to it.

T. J. Demos notes the dilemma that climate denialism poses for environmental activists. When we appeal to scientific expertise, we defer responsibility, giving up science to the dominance of states and capitals able to fund and deploy it; when we resist scientific expertise, we begin the slide into an inadvertent alliance with climate denialism, with the eco-thugs of extractive industry who spend billions to protect their interests by any means necessary. Demos argues, "Facing this dilemma, one must be aware of the fact that whatever we know about the environment—knowledge that will determine our future actions and chances of survival—we owe to the diverse practices that represent it" (18). The NHM locates itself at the site of these representational practices. Its wager is that insofar as science is shaped by a truth exterior to it, science cannot itself communicate its partisanship. Even as scientists are involved in practices through which they "fight to the death" or, in other words, in which they pursue and defend findings and methods as if their life depended on it, they tend to support a view of scientific practice as a whole as neutral and objective. Critics of corporate-funded science, industry-funded science, state-funded science, racist science, sexist science, and colonialist and imperialist science rightly and repeatedly demonstrate the falsity of this claim. All these particular enactments of scientific practice propel themselves by enclosing what is common within the limits enabling the practice. The practice of science is configured by its settings, settings to which it contributes. But the truth of science is not the same as the practice of science. To affirm this truth is to force a gap within scientific practice, making science the truth of a subject.

With a technique that might be described as overidentification or mimetic exacerbation, the NHM produces an elaborate staging not just of what natural history museums could be but of the form of the natural history museum promises. It promises a collective encounter with a world, a universe, a knowledge common even when distant

Figure 11. The NHM, *Will the Story of the 6th Mass Extinction Ever Include the Role of its Sponsors?*, 2015. Diorama in an exhibition at the American Alliance of Museums Annual Convention, Atlanta, Ga., depicting the David H. Koch Dinosaur Wing at the American Museum of Natural History in New York several hundred years into a dystopian future. Photograph by the NHM.

and unknown. It holds out the force of a truth that impacts and shapes us in ways that are unknown and unpredictable not because they are outside of or distanced from human representations, institutions, systems, and struggles but because they are indelibly inscribed within them. Such a truth can only be accessed indirectly, anamorphically, through the screen of the museum as a form faithful to its communication. Because it is tethered to this truth, the NHM doesn't invite cynicism. It doesn't try to mobilize doubt. On the contrary, it hails viewers (and, indeed, the museum itself) as likewise faithful to the truth, as those who would be and are outraged when institutions that communicate scientific knowledge are compromised and corrupted. The NHM takes the subjects of truth and organizes them as the subjects of a politics.

CONCLUSION

If the Anthropocene is a concept that sutures fields (a useful formulation from Elizabeth Povinelli), then the anamorphic gaze is a perspective that inscribes division and finds politics in the gap. The NHM models such a split, demonstrating how institutions are forms of collectivity that matter and that can be seized. Their missions, styles, structures, and personnel, their very form, can be conscripted into a service they may not know that they support. The NHM confirms the existence of a truth that its visitors already know such that this truth becomes something more than an individual hunch—something with symbolic registration. Their perspective, like the system itself, is already collective. The challenge is for whom: for individuated visitors or for partisans in organized political struggle? The NHM arranges collectivity, division, infrastructure, and truth so as to cut through the anthropocenic enjoyment of helpless fascination with the spectacle. Rather than remaining satisfied with the critique of the institution for what it excludes, for what it cannot say, the NHM identifies with and amplifies the collective desire that already infuses it. As an activist platform, it does the work of political organization. It doesn't get lost in cynicism, failure, melancholia, or the endless circuit of critique. It doesn't aim to democratize or pluralize. It doesn't aim to activate passive spectators but rather to organize active scientists and museum workers. The NHM enables them to take the side they are already on as it mobilizes natural history museums as politicized camps in a class war against the fossil fuel sector at the heart of the capitalist system. Targeting the institution it salvages a preexisting language and infrastructure, claiming it as a common resource. It thereby provides an experiment in seizing the state that can, and must, be replicated.

Jodi Dean is the Donald R. Harter '39 Professor of Humanities and Social Sciences at Hobart and William Smith Colleges in Geneva, New York. She is the author or editor of twelve books including, most recently, *The Communist Horizon* (2012) and *Crowds and Party* (2016). She is also a member of Not An Alternative.

Notes

1. An earlier version of some of the points developed here appears in "The Anamorphic Politics of Climate Change," *e-flux* 69 (January 2016).

2. My description here positions enjoyment within the economies of desire and drive. For a fuller account, see Dean 2006.

3. A wide array of contemporary thinkers, activists, and artists are working with the themes of climate change, extinction, and the Anthropocene. My aim is not to criticize a particular person or work but to name a current present to greater or lesser degrees in the larger conversation or cultural milieu that has resulted from the uptake of the Anthropocene as the name for a problematic within the humanities. Examples could thus include Kingsnorth; McKibben; Morton; Evans and Reid; Chakrabarty; Connolly; Wark; the contributions to Davis and Turpin; and many others.

4. For an overview of the wide array of artistic practices brought together under the umbrella of socially engaged art, see Thompson.

5. For an elaboration, see Badiou; Dean 2016b.

6. Carter and Smith include Not An Alternative in their "The Best of Art in 2015."

7. See also Bishop's (2012) critique.

8. See Dean and Jones.

9. See also the periodization in Raunig's and Ray's (2009) preface.

10. See Raunig and Ray.

11. See Rosler.

12. See Not An Alternative (2015).

13. See Geilung.

14. See "The Limits of Neutrality: A message from *The Natural History Museum*," Center for the Future of Museums (April 23, 2015). Available at http://futureof museums.blogspot.com/2015/04/the-limits-of-neutrality-message-from.html.

15. See "To the Museums of Science and Natural History—An Open Response," (April 16, 2016). Available at http://www.co2science.org/articles/V18/apr/museumletterresponse.php.
16. See Gills and Schwartz.
17. See Landsbaum.
18. See Not An Alternative (2015).
19. As stated on its website: http://thenaturalhistorymuseum.org/about/.

Works Cited

Badiou, Alain. 2009. *Theory of the Subject*. Trans. Bruno Bosteels. London: Continuum.

Bishop, Claire. 2012. *Artificial Hells: Participatory Art and the Politics of Spectatorship*. London: Verso.

Carter, Holland, and Robert Smith. 2015. "The Best Art in 2015." *New York Times*, December 9.

Center for the Future of Museums (blog). 2015. "The Limits of Neutrality: A Message from The Natural History Museum." April 23. http://futureofmuseums.blogspot.com/2015/04/the-limits-of-neutrality-message-from.html.

Chakrabarty, Dipesh. 2009. "The Climate of History: Four Theses." *Critical Inquiry* 35, no. 2: 197–222.

CO2 Science. 2016. "'To the Museums of Science and Natural History'—An Open Response." April 16. http://www.co2science.org/articles/V18/apr/museumletterresponse.php.

Connolly, William E. 2013. *The Fragility of Things*. Durham: Duke University Press.

Davis, Heather, and Etienne Turpin, eds. 2015. *Art in the Anthropocene*. London: Open Humanities Press.

Dean, Jodi. 2006. *Žižek's Politics*. London: Routledge.

———. 2012. *The Communist Horizon*. London: Verso.

———. 2016a. "The Anamorphic Politics of Climate Change." *E-Flux* 69 (January). http://www.e-flux.com/journal/the-anamorphic-politics-of-climate-change/.

———. 2016b. *Crowds and Party*. London: Verso.

Dean, Jodi, and Jason Jones. 2012. "Occupy Wall Street and the Politics of Representation." *Chto Delat* 10, no. 34. https://chtodelat.org/b8-newspapers/12-38/jodi-dean-and-jason-jones-occupy-wall-street-and-the-politics-of-representation/.

Demos, T. J. 2009. "The Politics of Sustainability: Art and Ecology." In *Radical Nature: Art and Architecture for a Changing Planet, 1969–2009, Barbican Art Gallery*, 17–28. London: Koenig Books.

Donovan, Thom. 2011. "5 Questions (for Contemporary Practice) with Not An Alternative." *Art21*, May 19. http://blog.art21.org/2011/05/19/5-questions-for-contemporary-practice-with-not-an-alternative/#.VAxzBvldWSo.

Evans, Brad, and Julian Reid. 2014. *Resilient Life*. Cambridge: Polity.

Fraser, Andrea. 2011. "From the Critique of Institutions to the Institution of Critique." In *Institutional Critique*. Ed. Alexander Alberro and Blake Stimson, 408–17. Cambridge, Mass.: MIT Press.

Geilung, Natasha. 2015. "Protesters Urge the Smithsonian Institution to Cut Ties with Climate Denier David Koch." *Think Progress*, June 15.

Gills, Justin, and John Schwartz. 2015. "Deeper Ties to Corporate Cash for Doubtful Climate Researcher." *New York Times*, February 21.

Kingsnorth, Paul. "Dark Mountain Project" (the self-published manifesto is available at http://dark-mountain.net/about/manifesto/).

Lacan, Jacques. 1998. *Seminar XI: The Four Fundamental Concepts of Psychoanalysis*. Ed. Jacques-Alain Miller. Trans. Alan Sheridan. New York: Norton.

Landsbaum, Claire. 2016. "Climate Denier David H. Koch Leaves American Museum of Natural History's Board." *New York Magazine*, January 21.

Lyons, Steve, and Beka Economopoulos. 2015. "Museums Must Take a Stand and Cut Ties to Fossil Fuels." *Guardian*, May 7.

McKee, Yate. 2013. "DEBT: Occupy, Postcontemporary Art, and the Aesthetics of Debt Resistance." *South Atlantic Quarterly* 112, no. 4 (Fall): 784–803.

———. 2014. "Art after Occupy—climate justice, BDS, and beyond." *Waging Nonviolence*, July 30. http://wagingnonviolence.org/feature/art-after-occupy/.

McKibben, Bill. 2010. *Eaarth*. New York: Times Books.

Morton, Timothy. 2013. *Hyperobjects*. Minneapolis: University of Minnesota Press.

Natural History Museum, The. 2016. "About the Natural History Museum." http://thenaturalhistorymuseum.org/about/.

Not An Alternative. 2015. "The Radical Subject of the Post-Apocalyptic Generation." In *The Art of the Real: Visual Studies and New Materialisms*. Ed. Roger Rothman and Ian Verstegen, 86–100. Newcastle-upon-Tyne: Cambridge Scholars.

Parenti, Christian. 2011. *Tropics of Chaos*. New York: Nation Books.

Raunig, Gerald, and Gene Ray, eds. 2009. *Art and Contemporary Critical Practice*. London: MayFlyBooks.

Rosler, Martha. 2011. "Lookers, Buyers, Dealers, and Makers." In *Institutional Critique*. Ed. Alexander Alberro and Blake Stimson, 206–35. Cambridge, Mass.: MIT Press.

Steyerl, Hito. 2009. "The Institution of Critique." In *Art and Contemporary Critical Practice*. Ed. Gerald Raunig and Gene Ray, 13–19. London: MayFlyBooks.

Thompson, Nato. 2012. *Living as Form: Socially Engaged Art From 1991–2011*. Cambridge, Mass.: MIT Press.

Wark, McKenzie. 2015. *Molecular Red*. London: Verso.

SIDES VIEWS SPLIT
(A RESPONSE TO JODI DEAN'S "A VIEW FROM THE SIDE")

Tony C. Brown

0. The original response I gave to Jodi Dean's characteristically incisive and committed presentation followed closely the written text of it Dean had kindly provided me several weeks prior to the symposium. The response I include here remains roughly what I said at the time, though with several alterations, first for clarity and second (with one exception noted below) for continuity in light of changes Dean has made to her text since the symposium—changes that Dean, again, shared in advance of my completing the response that now follows. I say all this by way of introduction, not only to give a sense of the favorable conditions under which I have been able to respond but to underscore Dean's openness to engagement, a quality that may at times seems missing in the polemical charge of her argument against what she calls anthropocenic enjoyment.

Dean demonstrates in her professional practice how one can be strident and committed and yet open and engaged. She exemplifies the importance of combining strident commitment with open engagement and shows us not to be afraid of mixing one with the other. Such lessons are important to bear in mind. They may help one avoid a possible misreading of Dean's argument. Her questioning of anthropocenism is not a rejection of climate change or of planetary damage due to certain actions by certain human beings. Rather, Dean's claim vis-à-vis anthropocenic talk is something like this: *the terms by which* it addresses planetary damage as caused by the human species, by humanity tout court, prevent effective responses to the damage. Particularly, they block effective criticism of, and action against, those individuals and institutions that continue to profit from the damage they continue to obscure or simply deny.

As a far better option, Dean offers The Natural History Museum (NHM) as a model of active and effective response. The project seeks,

Dean says, to "make legible" certain infrastructural aspects of natural history museums and in doing so pressure such institutions to acknowledge their own involvement in climate change and its dangers—and ultimately make the institutions themselves change, forcing them to acknowledge and address their own involvement in climate change and its dangers. The aim is hard to disagree with (though it does remain uncertain how an institutional change such as the one Dean describes—namely, the change in the American Natural History Museum's board of directors—intervenes in climate change). Still, what I suggest comes down to this: just as a figure disfigures, a making legible may at once make unreadable. And what becomes illegible, what is, as it were, being disappeared, has proper names like Tuvalu and Carterets.

1. Now, to respond, I will start at the beginning, or just before it, with the title of Jodi Dean's presentation, "A View from the Side":

  i. "a view": there would be more than one view, then, and what comes after the title will be one view among other possible views "from the side."
  ii. "the side": whatever the view taken, it is from *the* side. This will not be "a view from a side" among other possible sides; there is just the one side.

By the title, then, the initial opening of possible views (a view as one among other possible views) is quickly tempered and limited, there being just the one side from which to take a view. Following the title, yet still with the title—we have a subtitle—the side view to be taken is named "The Natural History Museum."

2. Beyond the title, it soon becomes apparent that "the side" is in fact split, meaning:

  i. on the one hand, "the side" as anamorphosis, on the model of Hans Holbein's *The Ambassadors* (to which I will return, but which Dean has already presented, saving me, at this point, the need to explain); and,
  ii. on the other hand, "the side" as a taking-sides-against, "the side" becoming the side of the partisan, the side of the one side as against the other that is not a side, the non-side of State-Capital-Nation, and most specifically, the full frontal of David

and Charles Koch and their fronting institutions (the American Museum of Natural History, the Smithsonian, etc.).

So there is just the one side, yet that side becomes two, and then almost four: the two sides of the pun, anamorphosis and partisan, and the two sides of the "taking-sides-against another side that is not a side," or "the side" and "the front."

3. The partisan view to be taken up is (as the subtitle suggests) that of The Natural History Museum, an ongoing project by the arts collective Not An Alternative, itself located on the side of the East River, or actually on one side of it, the east side, in Greenpoint, Brooklyn. Dean details, with great clarity, the ways Not An Alternative constitutes a serious concern. It is a long-standing, well-organized collective—so much so one could almost say it is an institution, though one that works by working at and in the margins of other, dominant institutions. Not An Alternative secures funding through various foundations and other sources, and it mounts significant, serious projects, which (according to its website) "have been featured within art institutions such as the Solomon R. Guggenheim Museum (NY), PS1 / MOMA (NY), Tate Modern (London), Victoria and Albert Museum (London), Museum of Contemporary Art Detroit, and Museo del Arte Moderno (Mexico City)." As this list of venerable institutions may itself suggest, the collective's seriousness carries over into its artworks, projects, and interventions. Not An Alternative does not rely, Dean notes, "on aesthetic gestures of critique, irony, or the retreat into poetic reverie. . . . *The Natural History Museum* isn't a joke or a stunt" (2016b). It is straight-faced, front on, and yet from the side. Of itself, Not An Alternative says (again, on its website) that it works "not through a typical head-on (or head-butt) approach, but through the occupation and redeployment of popular vernacular, semiotics, and memes."

4. The one word remaining from the title I have to address is "from": "A view *from* the side." At first glance "from" seems to be split like "the side":

i. First, there would be the view "from" the side disclosed by the NHM, as confirmed by the title's subtitle. This is the side we are looking at, from the front, with "the side" as our object.

ii. Second, there would be the view "from" the side Dean argues we should take as a matter of practice. This view means not just looking front on at the view from the side that is the NHM but looking from where the NHM is looking.

Here, with "from" (and so unlike "the side"), the first and second cannot be maintained at once, each standing in a relation of contradiction to the other. The second cancels the first. So the split of "from" is only apparent, and its unity in turn works to prevent any side-splitting (we are being serious, after all). The side becomes clearly just the one side: looking with the NHM, from the side that is at once "its side" and "the side."

5. Having determined who is looking at what from where, the determination will soon prove hard to maintain. Everything would be much clearer if one could just say "there is this side" and "there is that side," the opposition remaining stable and exclusive: there are the goodies, there are the baddies. As Jodi Dean indicates, such oppositions are hard to maintain in any purity—and they may just be politically debilitating anyway. Dean's partisans (much as Carl Schmitt said was the case for all partisans) cannot exist outside the forces of state/capital/nation. The partisan fights irregularly but remains dependent on, relies on, regularized political organizations. So too the NHM: it attempts to insert irregularity into regular institutions by way of regularized political or civil organizations (granting foundations, association membership, national museums, etc.).

6. Another source of perspectival uncertainty concerns the ability to distinguish what Dean says Not An Alternative does and what Not An Alternative says its does. The distinction proves hard to maintain rigorously, and not because what Dean and what Not An Alternative say may differ. The distinction is uncertain because Dean herself (according to Not An Alternative's website) has been a core member of the collective since 2010. The view Dean takes from the side that is the view of the NHM (looking at its looking from the side) is not necessarily distinct from the NHM's view (looking from the side). Still, whatever Dean's relation to the collective, her own view of it, or as it, seems at best partial. For in keeping with what seems the spirit of Not An

Alternative, the collective would have no one representative voice, while in her presentation Dean herself makes no claim to be speaking for it, and, in fact, avoided any mention of her membership.

7. If we have started to lose sight of stable separations we still get glimpses of some reassuringly familiar and predicable oppositions. The word Dean consistently uses to name what Not An Alternative does is "practice," a term also featuring in Not An Alternative's own literature. Over against the collective's practicing activism (PrAc), Dean presents a paralyzing anthropocenism (PaAn). Obviously, the opposition is not symmetrical:

    i. On the one hand, practicing and activist go together fairly easily—"activist" would seem to mean someone engaged in a "practice" of some sort: a practicing activist is an activist being an activist.

    ii. On the other hand, paralyzing and anthropocenist may appear to go together, and all too easily in current practice (and already here we are borrowing a term from the other side), yet the two do not necessarily go together in the way practice and activist do.

To underscore the nonnecessity of anthropocenic paralysis, consider anthropocenism's potential to motivate agitation and antagonism: it can be heard, at least in its stronger, almost apocalyptic versions, to deliver the ultimate "you have nothing to lose but your chains." Given that human life will end, and end without End (as in without purpose or final cause, just ceasing rather than arriving at an End), what reason could there be to continue accepting things as they are? Even if one embraced as beneficial for all (however appropriately reformed) the continued force of law and police, the continued ordering of life (human, animal, planetary, etc.) under contemporary regimes of capitalist production becomes clearly absurd. As we know, *die Scheidungsprozesse* of surplus value's so-called accumulation occasion, by their nature, bring much in the way of suffering and misery (most simply, the ownership by some of the means of production of all, but also Marx's various "lines of blood and fire"). But in the absence of any possible heaven, on earth or indeed in heaven, the mode of production we call capitalism stands exposed to a radical, existential contingency.

8. To the extent Dean identifies anthropocenic talk as just paralyzing, the asymmetry of her PrAc and PaAn opposition secures the identification. Or more precisely: a rhetorical shoring up casts the pair PaAn in the tautological hue secured by the pair PrAc (so that Pa is to An as Pr is to Ac), a shoring up that makes possible:

i. first, rendering as banal anything one may associate with an anthropocenic position; and,
ii. second, reserving positive practice and action to just the one side.

The message is clear: if you want to be an authentic doer, do not be an anthropocenist. We might even say (employing Henrik Ernstson and Erik Swyngedouw's phrase) that the imperative is: do not be an anthro-obscenist, though the problem with anthropocenists seems that they are at once too obscene and not obscene enough.

i. On the one hand, they enjoy the prospect of human extinction that will follow from the immensely destructive actions of human beings.
ii. On the other hand, they hide politics from view, refusing exposure to the scene of politics, to the infrastructural undersides of expropriation, accumulation, and so forth.

9. Of course, these same two hands shake each other in what Jodi Dean points to as PaAn's crucial misstep: the obscene blaming of all human beings for the impending destruction of all human beings and much else besides. Jodi Dean notes that such an approach hides climate change's differential effects: as she says, Bangladesh has more to worry about than Russia on the global effects front.[1] But we slip here on two fronts:

i. First, from blame (or cause) to effects: blaming every human being "[screens] out the unequal distribution of the effects of warming" (Dean 2016a). But whether or not identifying the cause of the disaster in the human as species is appropriate, it does not follow that blaming all human beings would preclude acknowledging some human beings will be more adversely effected than others.

ii. Second, we are slipping between two different timescales: from a long view of a still somewhat distant future (the time when no one will escape the effects, not even the Russians), to a short view of a present (and soon-to-be ever-more-present present) in which effects on different human beings and different human populations can still be unequal. Whether or not an anthropocenic position binds one to only looking at a future annihilation, it does not follow that conceiving a time to come with no possible politics means not being able to see any politics at any time.

10. A time or place beyond politics, and perhaps beyond a politics understood as necessarily human, is a possibility Dean seems unwilling to entertain. I would not want to explain (away) that unwillingness by reference to Dean's disciplinary affiliation (political science), for the insistence on politics all the time and everywhere is, I take it, a fundamental principle of her political (and not just academic, as in: discipline and career) commitment. This also means that, for Dean, an attempt to see a limit to politics, temporally or spatially, is depoliticizing. We see this logic at work in Dean's opposing of PrAc and PaAn.

i. On the one side, the side from which Dean takes a view, there is political engagement as what a practicing activist does.
ii. On the other side, the side that is not a side, there is the screening out of politics, the depoliticizing, as what a paralyzing anthropocenist does.

Accordingly, *political* does not belong here to just one of the two sides; it becomes the ground of any possible side, or simply, it becomes the front, what appears to include all that is. Specifically, the opposing of PrAc and PaAn follows by first identifying a quality belonging to one of the two (PrAc's being political) and then installing that quality as the ground governing the identity of both, at which point the one can said to be properly grounded (it is political) and the other a perversion (it is depoliticizing). By the terms of the opposition, then, we can only not be political by subtraction: if we are not engaged politically, if we do not face up to politics and the political, we are depoliticizing, a negative that does not negate the positive, as the positive remains what really is, everywhere and at all times. Here, rather, the negative is a failure to engage and recognize what really is and in such a way as to lessen that reality.

To help make the logic clearer, let us imagine ourselves as Spinoza's talking triangle and say that everything is, by necessity, properly triangular, so if anything fails to recognize or embody its triangularity, that thing must be vainly detriangularizing. So, for example, being a square would not mean being a square but being a perversion of triangularity. The point I am making is this: in taking a contingent quality (political, triangular) to be a necessary or essential one (as Aristotle did vis-à-vis the human with political, and as Plato did vis-à-vis the universe with triangular), we produce as defective whatever remains contingent to the necessary order we claim *by our definition* (all is political, all is triangular). By definition, then, anthropocenic talk belongs to but denies politics, PaAn being the reverse of Not An Alternative's PrAc, though not simply as one positive pole over against another positive pole. Whereas PrAc insists on politics' primacy, what PaAn does in failing to do is depoliticize, and doing it so badly as to be paralyzing. Its apocalyptic strains appear as an action-sapping indulgence in empty gestures that serve to depoliticize what is always politics by no other means.

11. Claiming politics as the inescapable ground of human existence often enough assumes politics as the end of all action, of all thought, of all explanation, and so on. And note the slippage from human existence to all action, all thought, all explanation, all themselves understood as necessarily human: here, politics as always and necessarily human would become the End of all things, the governing final cause. The anthropocenic offers us the vision of a rather different end, and not only in the sense of a ceasing without purpose. Somewhat paradoxically perhaps, anthropocenism

    i. suggests the human has made itself a God-like force of nature, having developed, employed and expended, over the last two hundred years, such power as to alter the planet geologically and to such an extent as to make human extinction possible; and,

    ii. shows the human to have elevated itself to a force over nature by way of degrading everything else, a degradation legitimated by the human's assuming itself to be the world's purpose and the measure of all value on earth (as Kant wrote at the beginning of the Anthropocene, if there were a world without human beings, "so würde das Dasein einer solchen Welt gar keinen Wert haben" [320]).

If we wanted to square the paradox, we could say both entail exposing the human to a radical finitude (its extinction, it is not all there is, and it is not the point of all this is). But it should at least be clear, in following the anthropocenic logic as we have, that one major aspect of Dean's problem with it stands: its blaming all human beings for the coming end of all human beings and so much more. Though we would also have to say it ends up not too far from Dean in this sense: it assumes the end of all action as a human existence that becomes the cause of all existence.

12. I want to head toward a conclusion by considering differential causes and effects—what we could also invoke as uneven development, which is to say, uneven expropriation and accumulation. Although Jodi Dean includes a sense of unequal distributions of blame in her account of the NHM (David Koch claiming more than most), missing is what we might call global blame or cause. And I do not mean "missing" in the common academic sense of "you left out what I work on." I mean it somewhat as Dean uses the term: as what we look straight at but cannot make out because we are not looking from the side. So in the case of Holbein's *Ambassadors*, we cannot recognize the death's head, though it is there already in the full frontal view—and in fact it is there even without the anamorphosis, in the series of objects that figure, as Lacan notes, "les symboles de la *vanitas*" (101–102) (which we might consider as a sixteenth-century version of "you have nothing to lose but your chains"). That you think death is just to the side of life, on the sinister side, that is the joke of the anamorphosis, why it winks at you as you leave the room on the left: I have been right in front of you, looking straight at you, the whole time, always waiting for you.

13. In terms of global cause as "missing," the point would be that as long as "the side" remains only the east or right side of the East River we risk screening out exactly the side from which the view is being

taken and hence too quickly installing as necessarily true what is a one-sided position. Put another way: isolating *an* enemy against which (or here, against whom) to mobilize the people narrows our focus to just *that* enemy, and so hiding others (ourselves, for example) but also the capitalist state and global capitalism. Clearly this is not merely navel-gazing self-indulgence; if anything, it would be a turning to the side of such indulgence. Returning to Dean's title, if one were to insist on taking the predicate as transitive, and so expect "the side" to be named, we run into various possibilities, the United States being just the most obvious. But if we take a view from the side of the planet, namely the Global South, *nous sommes tous Kochs.* Not everyone (that is, not *anthropos*), but, among certain others, us here and now, on the Minneapolis Campus of the University of Minnesota, in Room 135 of Nicholson Hall on the east side of the Mississippi River, on this Saturday afternoon, at this moment when someone is saying we too are part of the problem.

It is not just that Bangladesh and atoll or island states like Tuvalu, Kiribati, Vanuatu, the Marshalls, the Maldives, parts of Papua New Guinea, and other areas of the south we now call global will be unequally affected: the people of Tuvalu, like the others, barely participated in causing what will for some time affect them worse than those in Russia—or those of us here in the United States. The point is: the question of global causes (and so of who to blame, who to stop) remains crucial insofar as the blamable actions—the causes, including obscenely excessive meat-eating and car-driving habits—remain in effect, practiced every day, and, as we know, practiced unequally, causing suffering that barely touches our otherwise affluent consciences. At the risk of thoroughly enjoying myself, let me repeat nothing new: even if we do not indulge in the Kochs' Fifth Avenue penthouse level of luxury, *our* continuing to lead the luxurious lives so many of us do continues to cause the total evacuation of the Carterets Islands as its atolls go under. This is what we might be looking straight at and yet still be missing. The Kochs have to be stopped, yes, and so do we.

Tony C. Brown is associate professor in the Departments of Cultural Studies and Comparative Literature and English Language and Literature at the University of Minnesota. The author of *The Primitive, the Aesthetic and the Savage: An Enlightenment Problematic* (Minnesota, 2012), as well as essays on Joseph Conrad, Marx's primitive accumulation, North American burial mounds, and aesthetic theory, he is currently working on a book manuscript entitled "Statelessness: On Almost Not Existing," which examines the role of those without a state in Enlightenment political philosophy.

Notes

1. I refer to passages read by Dean at the Symposium but not included in the version published in this issue of *Cultural Critique*. I retain my response to these passages as Dean has published them in an alternate version of her text, "The Anamorphic Politics of Climate Change," which makes the same argument using more or less the same material.

Works Cited

Dean, Jodi. 2016a. "The Anamorphic Politics of Climate Change." *E-Flux* 69 (January). http://www.e-flux.com/journal/the-anamorphic-politics-of-climate-change/.
———. 2016b. "A View from the Side: The Natural History Museum." *Cultural Critique* 94 (Fall).
Ernstson, Henrik, and Erik Swyngedouw. 2015. "Framing: Rupturing the Anthro-obscene! The Political Promises of Planetary and Uneven Urban Ecologies." Conference at Teater Reflex, KTH Environmental Humanities Laboratory, Stockholm, September 16–19. Position Paper Version 2. http://uct.academia.edu/HenrikErnstson.
Kant, Immanuel. 1968. *Kritik der Urteilskraft*. Ed. Karl Vorländer. Hamburg: Felix Meiner. (Orig. pub. 1790.)
Lacan, Jacques. 1973. *Le Séminaire, Livre XI, Les quatres concepts fondamentaux de la psychanalyse*. Ed. Jacques-Alain Miller. Paris: du Seuil.
Not An Alternative. 2016. "About Not An Alternative." http://notanalternative.org/about-us/.

END NOTES

Simona Sawhney

He woke up from the dream, pulse stumbling, stuttering, mouth parched—his body smarting from a forest of blows. In the dream, his old, battered Maruti had screeched to a halt as the police van thundering behind had swerved right in front. He had been dragged out on the road, as ramshackle traffic roared and hissed around him. The moon hung a feeble orb over the rancid night air. They had wrenched open the containers in the trunk. The squeal of a lackey: "It seems to be beef, Sir . . ." Blows, kicks . . . "Don't you know the law, you sister-fucker? But you won't learn this way . . . wait till we teach you a lesson . . ." Spine, knees, groin on fire . . . raging pain . . . . "You will eat the cow-mother, will you, will you, you bastard son-of-Babur?"

"Let me go, Sir," whimpering, sobbing, crawling . . . "You are mistaken Sir, you are mistaken, I have never eaten beef in my life, this is not beef." "What is it then, sister-fucker, if it isn't beef?" "It is not beef, Sir, it is . . . only . . . only . . . human-meat, Sir . . . flesh of some useless human beings." That look on the policeman's face, his lathi suspended in mid-air—idiotic, incredulous, disappointed. "Human beings?" He spat out the word with great globs of disgust. Then, suddenly, cunningly: "What was their caste, Asshole, what were their names?" He woke up.

If you're a foreigner, of course, you may eat beef.[1] And that is as it should be. Because foreigners have lifestyles, food preferences, tastes and habits . . . and hell, we've always been ready to cut up and serve our mothers, whether bony or bonny, to the guy who lands from afar with a thick wad of cash. Especially if he be fair of skin. If dark, then it's a different matter of course. Because the dark ones, don't you know, they fuck anything that moves. That must be the reason they all have a strange smell about them . . . or maybe it's the drugs. Prostitutes and addicts. They ought to be dragged out on the street and stripped, every single one of them.[2] But we're too tolerant, that's our problem.

That's why they all take advantage of us. So hospitable, so tolerant, so accommodating, that is why we are so abused. But enough is enough, right? No more niceness for these drug-pushing fornicators, these child molesters, these crazy beasts. They should go back where they came from. We will *send* them back, right back where they came from.

Now the fair ones, the blue-eyed ones, glowing and gorgeous with the pure sheen of pure wealth—they are a different matter altogether. Clear as day, they were born to rule the earth. Yes, yes, I know, we booted them out, our Great Leaders booted them out a few decades ago, but truth to tell, we've been yearning for them ever since the day they boarded their ships and left our shores. We yearn so much, so longingly, so wistfully, we spend all our time trying to adore them, emulate them, *become* them—only in flesh, mind you, only in flesh . . . I ask you, is it not grossly unfair to be ugly, if you could be Fair and Lovely instead?³ It is time we seriously put our minds to the Whitification of our beloved Motherland. White is the American, our younger brother, White the Truth, and White the Cow. And White indeed, indeed, was our Lord, though playfully, jestfully named Krishna, the darkie, by his blessed mother.

So, in the midst of this Grand Project of Whitification—blazoned on billboards and painfully etched on the skin—in the midst of this project of de-Beastification, which has strangely, paradoxically, morphed such that what is yanked out of the human is not the savage, violent beast, but instead the cud-chewing, ruminating, slow-gazing, unperturbed beast—in the midst of such projects, what on earth happened to one Rohith Vemula?⁴

On Earth. On the earth he too had lived. And on the earth, though suspended by a few feet, he died, making in the process the earth his theater.

Did he die because, in this sprawling world of uncountable spaces, we made sure that a Dalit who claimed freedom, who laughed aloud with open mouth, who strode with the bold spring of power, would be surely, inexorably pushed out of all possible spaces, one by one? Out of the public space of the university, out of the hostel, out of the blood-heavy air of nationalist piety?

Yes . . . and at the same time, no. For though we jostled and pushed and repulsed him at every turn, he finally left of his own accord, and that we cannot take away from him. He made a decision to leave.

Rohith Vemula's last letter, about which so much has already been written and said, is nothing so much as a testament to this final, irrevocable *decision*—a decision that doubtless implicates us all, and yet makes clear that in the last instance, the act was authored and signed by Vemula himself.[5]

What are we—what is the world—charged with in the letter? For there is certainly a charge, an accusation we cannot miss. Even though the letter begins not with an accusation but with a plea, a tender appeal to those who loved him, and who might, therefore, face in his departure the unworthiness of their love, and even though it says that Vemula has "no complaints," it is nevertheless clear that it also presents us with an accusation. In the very problems that Vemula had "with himself," we are already involved and implicated. What are we charged with? Not explicitly with discrimination, or casteism, or brazen brutality—though these are certainly our crimes—but with something perhaps more insidious, fundamental, and far-reaching: the refusal to recognize the other as a subject of thought. People become monsters when they are reduced, the letter says, "to their nearest possibility." Thought takes us far, it extends the range of human possibility, it reaches to the stars, in a spirit of curiosity, wonder, and love: "I loved science, stars, nature." For such a love, for such a thoughtful love, the love of science and stars, Vemula found no space. Most damningly, he did not find space for such love even in the university, which emerges from this event as a stunted, inhospitable institution, daily shrinking under the press of a stale, vicious nationalism.

The world saw him as a body, a mere body—and this is the way he indexes, obliquely, his Dalitness and the centuries-old reduction of the Dalit to a body without a mind. Cleaving a gap between his body and soul, the world made him a monster—that is to say, someone who is no longer able to concern himself with himself. It should be evident that in this context, to be concerned about oneself is not to be concerned about one's "immediate identity" or "nearest possibility"—but rather to be concerned about oneself as a thinking being, a thoughtful being, a being made up of distant dreams and strange thoughts. To be concerned about oneself is to be concerned about one's soul. When that concern withers away, there is perhaps nothing to live for.

Thus Vemula says, "I have become a monster," but was this last act indeed the act of a monster? Or was it not, rather, the only *thoughtful* act left for him, the only way he could put together again body and soul? For the act of killing himself must be seen as one with the act of writing the letter. The letter, the only "letter" to the world he was able to write, is inseparable from this act: together, the two vividly reveal the utter inhospitality of the university, not only to the Dalit, the Muslim, the rural, the outsider, but to thought itself.[6] Inhospitality in the name of the homeland and nativity—this is perhaps the most brazen and terrifying sign of our times.

The thought that the letter articulates: could it have been articulated without the seal of death? This is different from asking: would we have heard it without that seal, would we have heard it differently, would it have reached the media, the attention of international scholars, and so on? The answer to all these latter questions is obvious. But the question I wish to ask is somewhat different—namely, could the plea, the confession, and the indictment inscribed in this letter have found any means to appear, were they not framed and supported by Vemula's already changed relation to the world he inhabited?

It goes without saying that in no way do I wish to condone, or worse, celebrate the death on the ground that it yielded this letter; in no way should we think of this death as a sacrifice, not even as a sacrifice that enabled the writer's own thought. To think of this death as a sacrifice would be to pull it into a register of political calculation and, indeed, strategy—a register disavowed by the very language of the letter. For what does this language reveal if not a final, and hence most serious, focused attempt to concern himself with himself? It states: this is what I wanted, this is what I could not do. In the final hour, I face my failure, I face that which blocked my possibilities. Except that in Vemula's case, in the very stating of his failure, he perhaps overcomes it in a manner rarely granted to mortals. So we cannot, we must not, think of his death as a sacrifice—in doing so, we would pull it into the very register of nation-as-family, as patriarchal family, that Vemula seems to have consistently resisted in his quest for a political community of the unminored minor. Here I am thinking not only of his claiming of Dalitness via the maternal (a claiming of identity through and in solidarity with the mother), not only of his defense of the screening of *Muzaffarnagar Baaqi Hai*, but also of a Facebook post he wrote on November 28, 2015, which succinctly summarizes the problem with a certain entrenched conception of the political community, spanning both the

Right and the Left. "#If Communist parties are allegedly for the down-trodden, they say. Then why do they have 'Women wing', 'Dalit wing' and 'Minority wing?? Is it not self-explanatory about the composition of 'Skeleton' and 'Muscle' in its body??" In a party allegedly founded for the minor, in the name of the minor, the minor is nevertheless doomed to perpetually remain a "wing" of the body. I find it both intriguing and revealing that in this brief allegory of the political community Vemula invokes the "skeleton" and "muscle" rather than the "heart," as one might perhaps have expected. Could we not draw from this the lesson that the politics of the minor without minority will have to be a politics of bone and muscle, and no longer one of head and heart—that is to say, no longer one of the gendered and hierarchical figuration of the center (and the periphery)?

What is it that distinguishes the genre of the text that proceeds from a decision to kill oneself—namely, the suicide note? At the very moment when one announces that one is no longer concerned with oneself, no longer desirous to being in the world, such a note addresses the world, recasts one's life, and fashions an image to leave behind. This should not be seen as an instance of duplicity or confusion, even if, in the realm of language, a certain duplicity or confusion remains unavoidable. Instead, it may be that the relation between the act of suicide and the writing of the last letter offers a singular example of the relation between action and thought, deeds and words. This is a relation where thought and action each reaches to the lack inherent in the other, its fraught and always questionable significance, and attempts to assuage, in the most irrevocable and severe manner, the terrible loneliness of both thought and action. The letter needs the seal of death, in the same way as the death needs the letter as witness.

As we know, a period of time lapsed between the writing of the letter and the act of suicide; time during which one lingering trace of resentment, of bitterness against allies, was scratched out. At the end, no personalized resentment, only the "state of things" as Vemula saw it.

"I always wanted to be a writer. . . . I am writing this kind of letter for the first time. My first time of a final letter."

In writing the final letter—a final reach for freedom, for the dream of being a writer. Just as the act of suicide itself reaches for the last freedom left, the last decision granted to one, the letter reaches for the last chance of fulfilling an old ambition. "My first time of a final letter," says Vemula, perhaps ironically. The suicide note might differ from all other writing simply in that it can only be written once. The first time is (almost) always the final time. Irrevocably linked to mortality, the suicide note is itself the most finite, the most mortal of texts; there is no skill one can gain over time to perfect its writing. It offers, should the writer wish to grasp it, the strangest of opportunities: the fundamentally political opportunity to link one's decision to depart from the world with one's hope for the future of that very world. The words written at the moment of parting signal, before all else, the strength of the desire to address the world, for the first and final time, in a way that one was unable to do before. Such an address, even if it take the form of nothing but a scathing indictment, must, at some level, arise from a hope, and hence cannot be read as pure despair or pure defeat.[7]

Rohith Vemula, the antinational.[8] In his death he left us with much to think about birth, caste, nativity, the nation, and the home. The human being can only make the earth a home if she can also dwell among the stars. The earth is, and is not, our only home. It can only be our home as long as we remember that it is not our home. So far it has been the lesson of the secular to make the earth our only home and the lesson of religion to render it instead a wayfaring station, a resting place on a longer journey. But death, all death, and certainly, insistently, a death such as Rohith Vemula's—a poetico-political death that in one final, scratched-out, mortal, finite letter attempts to bring together body and soul—can be claimed neither by the secular nor the religious. The earth is indeed our only home, but we do not belong here. How can we recall and hold within ourselves this fundamental unbelonging that nationalism violently tries to repress; our suspension between the earth and the sky, which it stridently erases?

If the nation is the most ambitious attempt to render organic and spiritual a proprietary relation to the land, the rivers, the forests—and to render, in turn, the spiritual itself as a proprietary category—then Vemula was certainly antinational. His letter prompts us to find a new way of speaking about the earth, the stars, the soul and body—a way that neither the religious nor the secular has thus far been able to alight on and pursue. If the Dalit (in this sense, like the proletariat) is a category whose project is to destroy itself, to annihilate, indeed, the very frame that birthed it, then it perhaps has something particular and singular to teach us about the pain of belonging, the travails of identity-as-home, and the joyful affirmation of transience and unbe-longing. It was not Rohith Vemula but instead his opponents who seem to have drawn the line connecting the annihilation of caste with the annihilation of the nation. For us, the task is to draw and read that line in an entirely different way: recasting, first and foremost, all be-longing as that which can only arise because of a prior and essential unbelonging; and hence all hospitality as that which can only arise from first unhousing oneself. Such are the difficult thoughts and prac-tices that Rohith Vemula's first and final letter has bequeathed to us.

FULL TEXT OF ROHITH VEMULA'S LETTER

Good morning, [9]
   I would not be around when you read this letter. Don't get angry on me. I know some of you truly cared for me, loved me and treated me very well. I have no complaints on anyone. It was always with myself I had problems. I feel a growing gap between my soul and my body. And I have become a monster. I always wanted to be a writer. A writer of science, like Carl Sagan. At last, this is the only letter I am getting to write.
   I always wanted to be a writer. A writer of science, like Carl Sagan.
   I loved Science, Stars, Nature, but then I loved people with-out knowing that people have long since divorced from nature. Our feelings are second handed. Our love is constructed. Our beliefs colored. Our originality valid through artificial art. It has become truly difficult to love without getting hurt.
   The value of a man was reduced to his immediate identity and nearest possibility. To a vote. To a number. To a thing. Never was a man treated as a mind. As a glorious thing made up of star dust. In every field, in studies, in streets, in politics, and in dying and living.
   I am writing this kind of letter for the first time. My first time of a final letter. Forgive me if I fail to make sense.
   My birth is my fatal accident. I can never recover from my childhood loneliness. The unappreciated child from my past.
   May be I was wrong, all the while, in understanding world. In understanding love, pain, life, death. There was no urgency.

But I always was rushing. Desperate to start a life. All the while, some people, for them, life itself is curse. My birth is my fatal accident. I can never recover from my childhood loneliness. The unappreciated child from my past.

I am not hurt at this moment. I am not sad. I am just empty. Unconcerned about myself. That's pathetic. And that's why I am doing this.

People may dub me as a coward. And selfish, or stupid once I am gone. I am not bothered about what I am called. I don't believe in after-death stories, ghosts, or spirits. If there is anything at all I believe, I believe that I can travel to the stars. And know about the other worlds.

If you, who is reading this letter can do anything for me, I have to get 7 months of my fellowship, one lakh and seventy five thousand rupees. Please see to it that my family is paid that. I have to give some 40 thousand to Ramji. He never asked them back. But please pay that to him from that.

Let my funeral be silent and smooth. Behave like I just appeared and gone. Do not shed tears for me. Know that I am happy dead than being alive.

"From shadows to the stars."

Uma anna, sorry for using your room for this thing.

To ASA family, sorry for disappointing all of you. You loved me very much. I wish all the very best for the future.

For one last time,

Jai Bheem

I forgot to write the formalities. No one is responsible for my this act of killing myself.

No one has instigated me, whether by their acts or by their words to this act.

This is my decision and I am the only one responsible for this.

Do not trouble my friends and enemies on this after I am gone.

Simona Sawhney is, together with Cesare Casarino and John Mowitt, a senior editor of *Cultural Critique*.

Notes

1. The slaughter of cows and sale of beef is prohibited in most states in India. In February 2016, there were news reports that the government of the state of Haryana would be willing to allow foreigners to eat beef, though later these reports were retracted. http://indianexpress.com/article/india/india-news-india/haryan-beef-license-for-foreigners-govt-may-soon-issue-special-permits/.

2. A young Tanzanian student was beaten and stripped by a mob in Bengaluru in February 2016. Africans living in India routinely face brazen discrimination and violence.

3. "Fair and Lovely" is the name of a popular skin-lightening cream in India. It was introduced in 1975 and is exported to several countries, including Malaysia, Thailand, Sri Lanka and Pakistan.

4. Rohith Vemula was not quite twenty-seven when he killed himself on January 17, 2016. He was a PhD student in the field of Science, Technology and Society and the recipient of a junior research fellowship. Raised by a single mother, a Mala Dalit woman, he grew up in the town of Guntur in the state of Andhra Pradesh in circumstances that may be briefly, if inadequately, described as extremely difficult, both financially and emotionally. His deep interest in science and passion for reading took him as far as the PhD program. At the university, he read avidly about both Marx and Ambedkar, and developed a critique of the Left based on its neglect of caste. He became an active member of the Ambedkar Students Association (ASA), valued in the group for his bold arguments, his theoretical reach, and his fluency in English. On July 30, 2015, the ASA organized a protest against the hanging of Yakub Memon, a convict in the Bombay bomb blast case of 1993, fueling already simmering tensions with the Hindu Nationalist student group the ABVP (Akhil Bhartiya Vidyarthi Parishad). Tensions were further exacerbated when the ASA protested against the ABVP's disruption of the screening of Nakul Singh Sawhney's film *Muzaffarnagar Baaqi Hai (Muzaffarnagar Eventually)* at a college in Delhi University. The documentary is a searing indictment of the communal politics that erupted in horrific violence against Muslims in western Uttar Pradesh in 2013.

Growing hostility between the ASA and the ABVP in a context where the ABVP appears to have enjoyed the support of the administration and the political establishment eventually led to the discriminatory and uncalled-for expulsion of five ASA students from the hostel: Rohith Vemula, Sunkanna Velpula, Dontha Prashant, Seshaiah Chemudagunta, and Vijay Kumar. They had been staging a sleep-in strike on the university premises, sleeping in the open for fifteen days, before Rohith Vemula hanged himself on January 17, 2016. He had not received his fellowship stipend for six months. On December 30, 2015, the students had submitted a ten-page memorandum with details about their expulsion to former University Grants Commission chairperson Sukhdeo Thorat, but Vemula killed himself before Thorat could take action. Information about the events leading to Rohith Vemula's suicide may be found on many Internet sites, including these:

http://thewire.in/2016/01/19/the-chain-of-events-leading-to-rohith-vemulas
-suicide-19580/, and http://indianexpress.com/article/india/india-news-india/
behind-dalit-student-suicide-how-his-university-campus-showed-him-the
-door/.

Let me pause here to emphasize, in particular, three points foregrounded by this series of events: first, the growing power of the right-wing ABVP on university campuses across India, and its often violent attempts to block all criticism of Hindu nationalism; second, the ASA's forceful critique of the ABVP and its own articulation of political positions on a broad range of topics, including caste discrimination, violence against Muslims, and gender hierarchies; and third, the pivotal question of the death penalty in this context. Among those on death row, an overwhelming majority belong to Dalit, Muslim, or tribal communities. It is thus not surprising that the death penalty itself has emerged in recent controversies as the crucial site of the contest over the meaning and foundation of the nation.

5. The full text of the letter is reprinted at the end of this essay.

6. The reservations policy (an affirmative action policy) adopted in Indian educational institutions since 1990 has given rise to widespread resentment among the upper castes. While traditionally excluded groups (including the "scheduled castes" and "scheduled tribes") now have a better chance of entering these institutions, they often face staggering challenges—social, financial, linguistic—in their quest for an education. The promise of the law has been constantly resisted and undermined in ways big and small. A report by teachers of the University of Hyderabad, where Rohith Vemula studied, documents nine suicides by Dalit students between 2001 and 2013. Discrimination seems particularly vicious in departments of science and technology. After the suicide of Senthil Kumar (February 24, 2008), a doctoral student in physics in Hyderabad, the Senthilkumar Solidarity Committee listed "the exclusivity of 'pure science'" as one of the reasons for his death. Rohith Vemula had in fact moved from studying "pure science" to studying social science—he was in the Science, Technology and Society department. The exclusivity apparently persisted.

7. I take writing itself as a trace of hope: hope manifest as a defiant streak of lightning against the darkest of skies. Only such a hope can force one to utterance, rather than silence. Only such a hope could have possibly provoked even the most bitter and despairing remarks Vemula made. As when he wrote in a Facebook post in December 2012, after the death of the brutally assaulted and gang-raped "Nirbhaya": "In a nation like ours, death could be the only thing which can rescue us." Or when in a letter to the vice chancellor of the University of Hyderabad (December 18, 2015) he requests that a "nice rope" be supplied to the rooms of all Dalit students at the university or a "Euthanasia" facility be established. http://www
.india.com/news/india/dalit-euthanasia-rohith-vemula-letter-to-university-of
-hyderabad-vc-873626/.

8. In a pivotal letter written in August 2016 to the minister of Human Resource Development, Smriti Irani, Labour and Employment minister Bandaru

Dattatreya had described the University of Hyderabad as a "den of casteist, extremist, and anti-national politics," explicitly naming the Ambedkar Students Association in this context. See http://www.ndtv.com/india-news/read-minister-bandaru-dattatreyas-letter-to-smriti-irani-on-hyderabad-university-1267471.

9. Also available at http://indianexpress.com/article/india/india-news-india/dalit-student-suicide-full-text-of-suicide-letter-hyderabad/.

Review Essays

IN THE COLD NIGHT OF THE DAY
ON FILM NOIR, HITCHCOCK, AND IDENTITY

NIGHT PASSAGES: PHILOSOPHY, LITERATURE, AND FILM
BY ELISABETH BRONFEN
Columbia University Press, 2013

Markos Hadjioannou

This article originates from a certain philosophical interest in one of cinema's most elemental features: its dark side. Cinema is a medium technologically constructed as a constant interplay between light and darkness, between the opening and closure of camera and projector shutters, between the control of quantities of light waves within dark chambers and the chemical reaction of light-sensitive surfaces to these waves or their electronic recording by sensors, between bright screens and dark theaters. Beyond the technological, cinema is also about narratives, narratives that, at times, tell stories about dark characters, about sinister and evil antagonists that creep out of murky shadows uninvited and unexpected, who appear at night to haunt our dreams and affect the calmness of our day. It is about stories with entities who gain their forbidding powers in the gloomy veils of the night that offers them protection from the luminosity of the day; and about people who conspire for the creation of a new reality while hidden inside the shielding opaqueness of the night. What all this goes to say is that darkness and the night—or rather, the darkness of the night—becomes a connecting feature that moves us from the technicity of the medium to its produced works and their cultural reception, expressing an immanence within cinema's own reality.

What, though, is it that we can learn about this nocturnal darkness, and by extension, about the relationship between night and day? To be certain, the night has come to represent an array of sinister or fearful characteristics that could be understood, to some extent, as constant from one work to the next. From a more philosophical perspective, it has been interpreted as the temporal space of our fears for the unknown, the metaphorical origin of life before order set in, or the realm of unconscious forces forever lying dormant—yet present—underneath the surface of our consciousness. By the same token, the day has become a metaphor for the light we seek to shed on the truth we aim to discover, the truth about our world and ourselves. If we were to extend this reading into the realm of subject formation, social living, and cultural production, could we imagine these nocturnal and diurnal temporal demarcations—or chronotopes—also expressing the desires and powers of women and men? And, most importantly, are these demarcations clearly delimited, or do they express instead the ambiguities of time's flow, individuation, and the possibilities of artistic expression?

Like all conceptual formations, the *nocturnal* has its own history within the tradition of Western thought, artistic production, and social rites. In her recently published and translated monograph *Night Passages* (2013), Elisabeth Bronfen takes us through part of the rich complexity of this history, offering researchers a welcoming resource for the development of the nocturnal in numerous works from philosophy, literature, and film. In so doing, Bronfen's work reminds us of the importance that has been given to the night throughout the history of aesthetic, social, and philosophical frameworks, thus showcasing that a focus on this concept is a much-needed and overlooked practice in current research. She shows us how a specific temporal part of a twenty-four-hour period serves more than just a quantitative sum of those hours between sunset and sunrise. The night, as exemplified in Bronfen's work, becomes a qualitative category that expresses a certain social psychology linked to the fears and anxieties brought up by darkness itself, as well as the desires and aspirations connected to the dreams of the individual, all hidden from the normative surface—glaringly revealed in broad daylight—of a male-driven social reality.

As my current article was originally requested to be a review of *Night Passages,* I will spend some time going through the details of the book in order to highlight its potentials, as well as its theoretical weaknesses. Most interestingly for me as a film scholar, Bronfen's book falls within a group of recent publications in the past fifteen years that address Hollywood's midcentury series of crime thrillers posthumously referred to as film noir.[1] Moving from antiquity into the century of the cinematic medium, she expands her reading of the night and its potential as a theoretical and aesthetic construct with certain transcendental values, exploring how it can be applied to film noir as that staple example of cinema's representation of the night. This is, of course, not the first time this tradition within American filmmaking has been discussed in this way—that is, as an ultimately nocturnal film form whose aesthetics seek to reveal the darkness that lies dormant within all corners of modern society.[2] Indeed, as an undergraduate student navigating my way through film courses whenever possible, I was taught by both textbooks and professors that film noir was a type of film characterized by dim interiors, sporadically lit gloomy exteriors, and dangerously dark characters, all expressing a certain disillusionment with humanity, society's fears for survival, and the anxieties regarding social living that materialized during, and right after, the Second World War. Most importantly, though, film noir also connected this darkness stereotypically with the feminine, and this via the infamous character of the femme fatale. It is on this association that Bronfen focuses in her book, connecting the portrayal of the night to the history of the philosophical and cultural representation of women as both the bearers of change as well as the originators of sin, evil, and destruction.

Yet there is something within this debate that leaves me unsatisfied. Is the nocturnal just the darkness within which crime and the sinister reside, or where destructive change tends to happen? Indeed, many classic noir films have traditionally created a destiny for their female protagonists, through which the femme fatale will have to resort to violence, deceit, and malice in order to break away from the restricting forces of a male-centric normative society. My question, though, remains whether this representation of femininity is too reductive—a representation that restricts women to the concept of the nocturnal as a psychological state of a distressed mind seeking release from social subordination. Could we, instead, read the nocturnal as a signifier of temporal duration, a chronosign rather than a chronotope that creates the sense of a delimited spatial category? Could we see, instead, the nocturnal as a theoretical construct expressing a more complex array of social relations that see the feminine and masculine as tightly woven and interchangeable frameworks within the realm of creative production?

It is, indeed, the latter version of the night–day relationship that seems to have more potential in my view, a potential for a radical understanding of how night and day—the nocturnal and the diurnal as signifiers of a Bergsonian *durée*—have been interpreted and represented in cinema and *by* cinema as a technological medium. While film noir has become this category of very specifically chosen films that repeat similar narratives and aesthetic tropes, we do see films that expand the horizons of this tradition without fitting within it entirely. It is with this in mind that I will turn to the work of Alfred Hitchcock, and especially his 1943 film *Shadow of a Doubt*, which is a wonderful example of Hitchcock's directorial mastery, presenting us with an interesting comment on the film production of the time. As I will discuss further on, by bringing the debauched masculine agency of film noir head to head with the tormented feminine desire of the American melodrama, Hitchcock shows us that the conceptual specificities of women and men, chaos and order, and night and day can be overturned. In fact, repeating this approach in a number of his films, Hitchcock has presented us with a series of tormented female and criminal male characters that seek to disclose a quite different version of the nocturnal and the diurnal—that is, a different version of temporality where genre and gender relations do not fit within the fixed dualities of binary structures.

THE *NOIR* OF FILM NOIR

Much has been written over the years about classic film noir, though my purpose here is not to reiterate its historical origins or the sociocultural readings of the group by the relevant scholarship at length. Instead, my interest in film noir stems from the theoretical stakes of its treatment of the night and of femininity.

In general, film noir has come to describe a series of films that emerged in the United States from around 1941 until 1958, albeit with significant specimens appearing even earlier. What concerns me, though, from a theoretical perspective, is the very term "film noir," which makes apparent something quite interesting about *interpretation* as an analytic mode in itself—that is, about what constitutes *theory*. Indeed, we come up against a certain difficulty when wanting to theoretically define film noir, a difficulty that has become part of the scholarly and critical treatment of the relevant group of films and a matter to which it may, in fact, be worth paying attention.

Speaking about this theoretical uncertainty, James Naremore—a prominent figure in the discussion of film noir in recent years—reminds us:

> It has always been easier to recognize a film noir than to define the term. One can imagine a large video store where examples of such films would be shelved somewhere between gothic horror and dystopian science fiction: in the center would be *Double Indemnity,* and at either extreme *Cat People* and *Invasion of the Body Snatchers.* But this arrangement would leave out important titles. There is in fact no completely satisfactory way to organize the category; and despite scores of books and essays that have been written about it, nobody is sure whether the films in question constitute a period, a genre, a cycle, a style, or simply a "phenomenon." (9)

Indeed, what this goes to say is that film noir is a term used to collect somewhat forcefully, or at least loosely, a set of films characterized by some connection to Gothic aesthetics and narratives, to a general sense of social dystopia, films that belong to a variety of genres including urban crime thrillers, gangster films, and horror and sci-fi movies. The image they create of the American landscape is bleak and unforgiving, with their expressionistic use of lighting and low-budget productions cultivating through visual tropes a sense of despair and general distrust toward humanity, civil society, and governing powers. As such, it is easy to see how the French critics saw them as expressing what came to be understood as a *noir* cinema. These are films dominated by the night; that is, they are nocturnal, dark, bleak, and sinister. Nevertheless, within these common grounds, we see significant differences that say a lot about how the *noir* of film noir is treated each time, and how it may express a more expansive array of different possibilities.

Let us return to the aforementioned quote by Naremore. Here he creates a somewhat loose beginning and ending for the group with reference to *Double Indemnity* on the one side and *Invasion of the Body Snatchers* on the other. Yet it is clear that these two films that are supposed to signal a beginning and ending for film noir in fact signal the convergence of both similarities *and* differences in the group—even when it comes to their treatment of the *dark side*. For example, as an urban crime thriller, Billy Wilder's 1944 film *Double Indemnity* is set in Los Angeles where an insurance salesman, Walter Neff, falls for the charms of the beautiful—though criminally sinister—housewife Phyllis Dietrichson. Having fallen in love with Phyllis, Walter joins her in executing a scheme to murder her husband in order to profit from his insurance policy. By the end of the film, though, not only is the husband killed, but Walter and Phyllis turn on each other too, leading to their ultimate mutual murder. *Double Indemnity* creates, as such, a thoroughly dark picture of the American urban landscape consisting of businesses, corporate entities and individuals, and family homes and personal relationships.

Quite differently, Don Siegel's *Invasion of the Body Snatchers* is a 1956 sci-fi horror film set in the fictional suburban Californian town Santa Mira. Here, giant alien plant pods have been producing human duplicates that replace each one of the town's citizens with identical copies. While the alien duplicates are physically identical to their originals, they lack one basic human characteristic: emotion. When a local doctor, Dr. Miles Bennell, realizes what is happening, he—unsuccessfully—tries to convince authorities to intervene and rescue the town. Sadly, by the end of the film all of Miles's friends have been replaced by their alien counterparts, while Miles also discovers masses of plant pods being cultivated for a large-scale takeover of the country. We have, once again, a quite bleak vision of life in the United States, but this time the basis of the anxiety has to do with alien forces taking over progressively the lives of the everyday American public.

What this simple comparison shows us is that there are similarities between the films that belong within the noir group, with this nocturnalization playing an instrumental part in how they are experienced and interpreted. Their dissimilarities, though, are of equal importance: from the one film to the next we move from the midforties to the midfifties, we move from an urban landscape to a suburban one, we move from a crime thriller to a sci-fi thriller, and, very tellingly, we move from the source of evil coming from a devious femme fatale to nonhuman extraterrestrials acting through their botanic proxies. The difference in production year is indeed quite revealing, as we make a shift from the latter years of World War II—with the war having an immediate impact on both the social structures and internal economy of the United States—to the Cold War era that represents a significant change in the country's international political agenda and new variations of Americans' own perception of their relationship to the nation and the rest of the world. This goes to show that, while these films' nightly environment is used to express a similarly cynical portrayal of contemporary society, it plays a significant part in also showcasing a shift in how this darkness is expressed and to whom or to what it is connected.

In sum, the *noir* of film noir characterizes a certain affinity to, or dependence on, the nocturnal qualities of the night—a darkness that has been culturally connected to the fears that surface as a result of our inability to see clearly what lurks within the shadows around us or what lies behind corners, doors, alleys, and so on. It is a darkness that expresses our anxieties regarding the difficulty to foresee or understand what might lie ahead of us, a tension associated with radical changes and latent impulses that go against rational stability and normative behavior. It is a darkness that, as such, has been associated with deviousness, crime, sinister desires, malicious dreams, pathological acts, and social disarray. To what extent, though, is this interpretation of the nocturnal useful when we are faced with a diverse list of films of varying genres and narratives grouped together under the umbrella of film noir? This might be a tricky question to answer, especially given the amount of work that has been produced in order to uphold the relevance of the term. Film noir, it seems, gains its conceptual merits by way of a historical accumulation of film criticism and scholarship that sustains the term, exemplified, for example, in the encyclopedic meticulousness found in Alain Silver and Elizabeth Ward's *Film Noir: An Encyclopedic Reference to the American Style* (1979). The matter remains, though, that this relationship between these mid-century American films and the cultural treatment of the night is useful to the extent that it can remain open—available, that is, for a reinterpretation analogous to the serendipitous qualitative impulses of time in general.

THE FATE OF THE FEMME FATALE

Before proceeding to discuss Hitchcock's directorial reinterpretation of film noir's nocturnalization, I would first like to address the stereotypical formulation of women and men in a number of these noir films. What is it that we can understand about the representation of the dichotomy between the feminine and masculine as manifested in the construction of the femme fatale and her male co-conspirators/

victims? Bronfen, to whom I referred at the outset of this essay, offers us a first way into this topic. In *Night Passages* she focuses on film noir, which she sees as addressing more than any other cinematic type the relationship between the nocturnal and the diurnal, maintaining that classic film noir is "the cinematic genre par excellence concerned with nocturnal scenes as well as nocturnal states of mind that infuse the day" (24). She explains that her interest with film noir has to do with its investment in a social order that is involved in the exchanges between fate, on the one hand, and agency, on the other. To no surprise, she relates these impulses with the treatment of the feminine and the masculine in the series of films she discusses, proposing a binary structure that connects the dark forces of the night with the representation of women and the social order of the day with that of men.

In order to understand better how Bronfen arrives at this interpretation of the nocturnal and diurnal and of women and men respectively, it is helpful to look deeper into the theoretical backbone of her project. She takes as her lead a link she establishes throughout her book between the ancient goddess of the night, Nyx, who is developed in Hesiod's *Theogony* (c. 700 BC), and the Queen of the Night that appears in Emanuel Schikaneder's libretto for *The Magic Flute* (1791). Wielding her powers from deep within the dark shadows, Bronfen reminds her readers that the ancient Greek goddess Nyx (mother of death and sleep but also of light and day) represented the terrifying anxieties of primordial existence before the world appeared—that is, before it became available to our vision. She then discovers Nyx's counterpart in the Queen of the Night from the latter part of the eighteenth century, just prior to the French Revolution and the world that was born from the new status quo that followed. In this case, the Queen of the Night is this devious motherly figure that is the embodiment of the night and whose rival is the sun priest Sarastro. Acting through magic, deceit, worldly and spiritual transgressions, and musical and visual excess, the Queen tries—but ultimately fails—to keep her daughter Pamina within the dark realm of the night and to stop her from joining her lover Tamino within the safety of Sarastro's enlightened world of rationalism and wisdom. As Bronfen notes, Schikaneder's libretto narrativizes the opposition between a nocturnal and diurnal philosophy, itself becoming an emblem of modernity's victory over an ancient regime based primarily, in that epoch's view, on superstition and religion. Not only does this connection directly point to the victorious affirmation of reason as the primary mode of philosophical thought and social governance but it does so by positing the *light* of the Enlightenment as an essentially masculine regime—one that seeks to uncover the truth of the world around us through the visible, through what is available to the rational thinker's observational powers.

To be sure, Bronfen's book in its entirety presents an interesting illustration of a mode of thinking, one that shows the creative potentials of theory itself as a methodological practice structured as an interconnecting reflective and reflexive activity. As she explains, her reasoning for turning from antiquity to Schikaneder's libretto is that it allows her to foreground her main argument: that the modern conceptualization and aesthetic manifestation of the night was a construct of the Enlightenment project, which was aimed at ostracizing this temporality from the philosophical focus of the contemporary period, and by extension the future (2013, 2–3). Opposed to the modus operandi of the nocturnal—where the darkness of the night allows for unexpected forces to prevail and change to be perceived as potentially destructive—the Enlightenment turned to clear, calculable, and constant reason as the dominant form of exploration and research, both philosophical and scientific. At the same time, Bronfen depicts a broad connection between the philosophical, theological, and literary representations of the night leading all the way from antiquity into the heart of modernity. These representations narrativize, as such, an oppositional conflict between night and day, upholding certain characteristics centered on a feminine–masculine binarism. Through these cultural works, femininity itself is expressed as a feared opposition to the world of order, structure, and existential security—an opposite, that is, to the rationalism of the Enlightenment that becomes the fertile ground for the development of contemporary society.

Most interestingly, Bronfen's project succeeds in identifying how, for this masculine mode of rationality to become victorious, it had to retrace, refigure, and generally reproduce the very regime it sought to defeat and replace: the nocturnal through which a feminine mode of agency and empowerment was being represented. She finds that the Enlightenment project was directly implicated in resurrecting and forming the type of knowledge and subjectivity that was connected to this feminized regime of the night. As she explains, her book is invested in a very specific twist to the Enlightenment project, "one that explicitly gives voice to the alterity it seeks to contain, not to repress nocturnal knowledge, but to give it its due and acknowledge its legitimacy" (2013, 3). In trying to marginalize the belief system of an ancient world, where mystery and mysticism reign above all else, the Enlightenment in fact reemphasized the potential of this other form of thinking, feeling, and acting—a system of impactful affects and cosmogenetic powers.

From this standpoint, Bronfen identifies, as she puts it, an "unceasing dialectic between night and day," which comes to symbolize a philosophical battle that can be traced throughout the centuries but that finds its culmination in the anxieties that the Enlightenment sought to appease (2013, 3). Faced with the loss of a belief system that found comfort in some number of metaphysical beings—God(s)—the modern skeptic was now in need of a new form of solace, as she or he was faced with the inevitability of life in a world riddled with a sense of alienation, isolation, and fear. The rational thinking of René Descartes's observing and calculating subject becomes now a means of taking control over the ceaseless transformations of the world and relocating the subject within reality, albeit via a scientifically grounded affirmation. Most problematically, according to Bronfen, this newfound mode of rationalism was invested in keeping the fortuitousness of a feminine world marginalized and demonized.

To return to film noir, Bronfen sees Nyx and the Queen of the Night reappearing once again as another nocturnal woman, this time in the form of the female protagonist of the group of films—that is, of course, as the femme fatale. Belonging, as it were, to a nocturnal chronotope, the female protagonist finds her primary agency in darkness (poorly lit interiors, dim corridors, moonless nights, and unlit alleys) from where she plots some transgressive scheme. Her thoughts and actions take on a transgressive potential in that they originate from a desire for her to free herself from a social role that has been forced on her—a role that connects back to the normative rationalism of the Enlightenment. Indeed, this transgressive act on the part of the femme fatale is done with a violent disposition that, more often than not, turns against both herself and her unknowing conspirer. The femme fatale manages to gain power through her machinations *of the night,* using her social marginalization to remain hidden while deceiving a man *of the day,* so to speak, into collaborating with her in order to bring some criminal act to fruition. This diurnal man is quite often a man of the law or a detective seeking the objective truth—a representative, that is, of the Enlightenment—who is lured into the femme fatale's malevolent embrace out of desire for that *other* world she comes to symbolize. This male agency, though, that originates from within the day, will find its fatal end in the uninhibited happenings and unexpected dangers of the femme fatale's world: the night.

To be sure, Bronfen's decision to work through the structures of film noir is undeniably justified given that this type of film leaves the impression of a world wrapped in darkness. Film noir's mise-en-scène can easily be seen to construct a *monde noir*—a dark world *of the night*. Moreover, the stereotypical roles ascribed to the female and male characters in many of the noir films work well with the equivalent female and male structures as described by Bronfen in her treatment of the nocturnal and the diurnal. It seems, though, that this approach is too restricting if we are to consider the variety of alternatives available to us from the filmic production of the time.

To begin with, we have here a group of films that is specific to a fixed historical period. Furthermore, noir films made up but a small portion of Hollywood's cinematic production during this time, and thus can hardly be seen to represent a totality of representational trends within audiovisual culture in general. Peculiarly, though, Bronfen does not pay attention to other successful genres from the time, and most importantly the horror film with an abundant list of examples—the Frankenstein, Dracula, vampire, and mummy movies, among others—appearing during the thirties and forties. Here we have a genre where the dangers and fears of the night indeed prevail and seep into the safety of the day, but where the source of evil is more commonly masculine. More so than this, she neglects to explore alternative trends of noir films, with Alfred Hitchcock's work presenting an intriguingly interesting alternative to the formations of the group.

NOCTURNAL ASSEMBLAGES: WO(MEN)

Even if we were to stick to classic film noir, it would seem more useful to think of the femme fatale as expressing a character of continuous transitional acts rather than of delimited formulas. Take, for instance,

Kelly Oliver and Benigno Trigo's recent book, *Noir Anxiety* (2003), where they point out how critics have interpreted film noir as representing changes within the patriarchal social structures of the United States. As they clarify, "These critics identify this breakdown of patriarchal authority as the source of the anxieties and fatalism of noir. They interpret the sense of fate or doom in film noir as a response to white men's sense of a loss of control and authority, especially control and authority over women" (xiii). These films, in other words, echo in both audiovisual and narrative terms the offset of a new social order where the stability of gender roles is seriously tested. The patriarchal authority of the enlightened subject of reason is now weakened as it finds itself living a new reality where women both express and enact different desires and needs: for emancipation, for an entry into the workforce, and for sexual freedom.

It is this observation that becomes the inspiration for Oliver and Trigo's argument, which sees the noir style as an expression of an overall anxiety linked to the very boundaries of identity as such being undermined (xiv). In sum, they see the conventions and formulas repeated in the films—among which the construction of the femme fatale and her male collaborator/victim—as a defense mechanism against the ambiguity of borders understood broadly as the limits of the nation, of race, and of sexual identity. Most importantly, the two authors see this attempt at creating identities in the noir films as one that flags up the very falsity and impossibility of the procedure—a weakness, as they explain, that "also drains identity of meaning, creates holes or vacuums at its center, and produces the anxiety that haunts film noir" (211). Film noir, in other words, attempts to create a world whose origins still lie in a realm of boundaries, where identity formation is still a clear-cut construct. Yet the reality of these films points out that these boundaries are continuously transgressed, making for a series of symptoms to appear: a series of *noir* sentiments linked to anxiety, fear, paranoia, and fatalism.

This approach is not far from that followed by Jonathan Auerbach more recently in his book *Dark Borders* (2011). Like many others, Auerbach turns to an interpretation of film noir's darkness. Here he argues that even though the films are not outwardly concerned with national politics, their aesthetic style and plotlines dramatize a general sense of political alienation (2). This alienation is one that corresponds quite directly with the historical period during which many noir films were produced, a time when the American nation was in the midst of the Cold War, dealing with threats from both inside and outside of the country and in need of redefining both a sense of nationhood and citizenship. Once again, in other words, the films are seen to express a battle between the need for delimited forms of identity and the awareness that this is no longer possible in a world already in the midst of global fluidity and national transgressions. As such, the uncanny qualities of noir's nocturnalization—and by extension of the main character of this feature, the femme fatale—become a filmic manifestation of a recognition of the national *other,* an *un-Americanness* threatening the boundaries of an American national ideology (3).

What we see in both these books is a desire to think of the *noir* of film noir and of the characters that have come to represent the group as expressions of a broader problematic—one that recognizes the gradual breakdown of identity formations at large. In the midst of this, structures of gender and their in-between relations are performed as much more malleable than what Bronfen recognizes, so much so that the character of the femme fatale and the femininity she represents is one that cannot be seen outside of its entangled assemblage with that of her male counterparts. It is indeed with this in mind that I arrive at Hitchcock, as it appears he was not only very aware of the aesthetic conventions of these gritty dystopian films, but that he was also interested in appropriating some of the group's conventions in order to lay bare an image of human relations that shifts the normative representation of women and men quite openly. Hitchcock, that is, offers us a truly fascinating alternative to gender representations, with an oeuvre that seeks to present a crisis of both the feminine and the masculine, a crisis that engulfs them both and packs them together in interesting and flexible ways. He presents us with worlds where gender—and genre—stereotypes are contested, explored, mocked, or put under threat.

SHADOW OF A DOUBT

While he does not belong to noir filmmakers strictly speaking, Hitchcock's work is, at times, inspired by both the themes and the aesthetics of this tradition. A notable example is his 1943 film *Shadow of a Doubt,* a film that self-consciously thinks through, and renegotiates, the staple characteristics of film noir, at the same time introducing a bridge between that tradition and the classic Hollywood melodrama.[3] The film opens on a calm neighborhood street in Philadelphia and slowly moves into the bedroom of a boarding house, where we find a man lying on a bed deep in his thoughts. This is Charlie Spencer, a man who, as we will find out much later in the film, has been making his living by seducing recently widowed rich women, referred to characteristically as merry widows, and then murdering them for their money and possessions. He believes that they deserve this morbid end because they are unworthy women who have taken advantage of their husbands' hard-earned wealth, wasting it on their own personal adornment and entertainment. He himself feels cheated by a society that leads him to financial hardship while the merry widows just fall into riches and happiness as a result of the hard work and ultimate demise of their husbands. As such, Charlie chooses to play a similar social game, taking on the role of a seducer much like the femme fatale, luring the widowed women into his charming arms only to lead them to their own ultimate night: their death.

While this leads Charlie to some prosperity, law enforcers are clearly catching up to him. Outside his rented room, standing in broad daylight are two investigators who have been tailing him. He realizes that it is now time to quit this criminal and deadly game and reaches out to his sister who lives happily with her family in a suburban neighborhood in Santa Rosa, California. His desire now is to enter into the domesticated safety of the home environment, far from the urban city streets, away from his current villainous life and its subsequent perils. He wants, in other words, to enter the social haven of the suburban family unit.

What makes Hitchcock's film quite radical—thanks also, of course, to Gordon McDonell's original story and the screenplay by Thornton Wilder, Sally Benson, and Alma Reville—is that we find another version of Charlie in the film, indeed situated at the opposite pole of his whereabouts and desires. This is his niece, a young woman with the same name as her favorite uncle. Both uncle and niece share an intimate fondness for the other, so much so that they seem to maintain a certain spiritual (somewhat incestuous) bond. More so than this, what is quite intriguing is that each Charlie is a sort of mirror reflection of

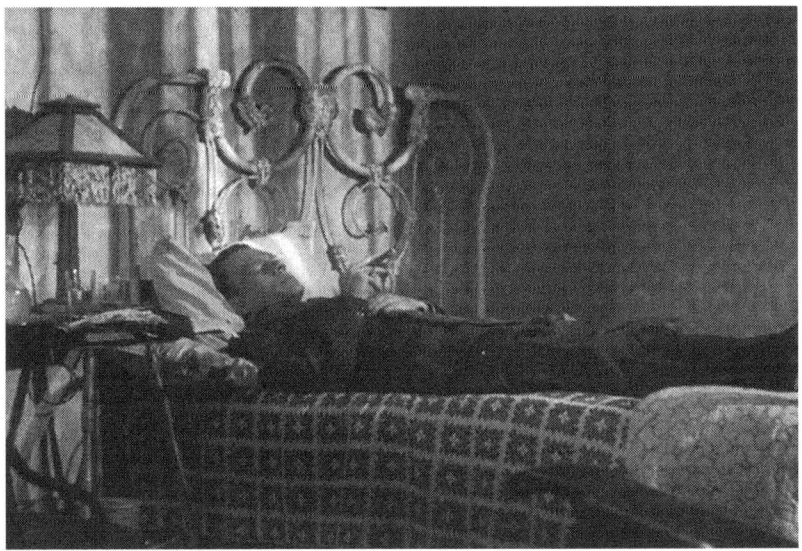

Figure 1. Uncle Charlie as the fatal noir character. *Shadow of a Doubt*.

Figure 2. Little Charlie as the melodramatic daydreamer. *Shadow of a Doubt*.

the other, an idea developed by Hitchcock's aesthetic construction of the two establishing scenes with which he first introduces the two characters.[4]

As opposed to uncle Charlie, who we find initially lying on a bed in an isolated and dim rented room, little Charlie is first seen lying in her own bed in a brighter bedroom, though similarly sunken in thoughts. The important difference is that, where uncle Charlie's fear of the law and punishment will lead him toward the interior of the house, little Charlie—much like her female counterparts in many melodramas—has her eyes on the world outside the home, a world she considers to promise blissful excitement, unlimited potential, personal growth, and social importance.[5] She sees her own mother with some disgruntlement, as she represents all that little Charlie does not want to become: a house-wife tied to her house, her husband, and her children. Little Charlie longs for the life in a big city, where she can live independently, exploring life much like her uncle—or so she thinks. It is precisely this domestic setting and the desire to break free from its constraints that bring us to the heart of the "women's film": the melodrama.[6] These constraints are expressed both in the house itself that keeps the mother and daughter enslaved within its walls, as well as the societal demands of a domesticated womanhood that is structured forcefully through preconceived norms. Thus, as Hitchcock presents the masculine Charlie of the film noir desperately climbing out of the darkness that he himself has built around him out of greed—a greed, let us not forget, that has as its victims women of high social status—he also offers us the antithesis of this in the form of the melodramatic heroine, the feminine Charlie. In contrast to her uncle, she is to be found in the luminosity of the day wishfully willing for the urban reality of the outside world—even if this is a world still dominated by men. The doubling effect, in other words, is quite fascinating, as it creates an initial dichotomy between uncle Charlie and little Charlie, representing here the relationships man-woman, night-day, film noir–melodrama, death-life.

Nevertheless, as *Shadow of a Doubt* progresses, the gender relations are complicated further. Uncle Charlie tries to tempt little Charlie with the riches of his way of living through a ring that he gives her, which belonged to one of the widows he had murdered. Like many of Hitchcock's mysterious objects that hold dangerous secrets about crimes and villains, the ring becomes a source of little Charlie's suspicions:

curious about an engraving on the gifted ring, as well as uncle Charlie's extreme reaction to a newspaper article he would not let her read, little Charlie seeks out answers in the local newspaper. Here she finds the announcement of an investigation regarding a murdered widow whose initials match those of the ring. In other words, through the act of careful *observation,* little Charlie pieces things together and realizes that uncle Charlie is actually the murderer of the merry widows. It is she who will become the investigator within the film's plot; she becomes the character, in other words, in search of the objective truth, thus taking on the role given traditionally to the male character in classic film noir.

Little Charlie thus gains a certain power over her uncle through the knowledge of his criminal secret. This knowledge becomes, though, the source of a fatal risk for her life, as uncle Charlie threatens his niece and attempts to kill her multiple times. Unlike the moral principles of the Enlightenment, in other words, *truth* becomes a life-threatening matter; it becomes the source of danger for existence itself. And yet little Charlie's psychological strength and wit manage to drive uncle Charlie out of town; and in a final battle between the two of them on a departing train, the young woman pushes her uncle to his death, killing him in self defense. The clash between the melodramatic heroine and the noir hero comes to an end, with the corruption of the man's dark criminality being destroyed by the sincerity of the woman's virtuousness and dedication to the well-being of her mother, her family, and her hometown. Once she has been saved from her uncle's villainous ways, though, her initial desire to leave the safety of a normative social structure that keeps her stuck in a suburban familial version of femininity come to an end as well. This is what seems to be implied in the last scene of the film, where we see her and one of the official investigators, Graham, standing outside a church like a couple ready to be married. By being paired up here with a law enforcer, in other words, little Charlie succumbs to a male-driven social order, following in the footsteps of her mother and other like-minded women.

Hitchcock's achievement is indeed noteworthy, offering us a reversal of film noir conventions by creating an intersecting dialogue between its nocturnal world and the brighter, yet equally problematic, reality of the classic melodrama. It is as if the darkness of the film noir finds its way into the brightness of the domestic home, where it slowly nests in an attempt to make it its own. By the same token, the glossy surface of the suburban home that is the central focus of the melodrama becomes now a cracking façade of a utopian edifice, in which we find sinister people, criminal behaviors, and unexplored and unsatisfied desires. The masculine Charlie is clearly a man of the night, a tempter who seduces women for his own gain. He is the male hero of the film noir insofar as he performs crimes for some personal gain; but he also takes on the role of the femme fatale by luring the widows sexually and leading them to their death. What is more, by wanting to go and join his sister in her home in Santa Rosa as a way of saving himself from his felonious life, he is also after the position of the melodramatic heroine who remains shielded by the suburban domestic haven.

The feminine Charlie, on the other hand, presents us with her own role reversals. She is the one who is initially seduced by her uncle's way of life, desiring to join the world of the urban social dweller. Faced, though, with her uncle's potentially sinister past, she quickly takes on the masculine role of the noir investigator, discovering the truth about the crimes. She becomes, in other words, the active agent, guardian, and explorer of knowledge. In fact, women who know or who seek out knowledge are quite prominent in Hitchcock's films, though their access to information is usually a dangerous privilege: from Miss Froy, for example, in *The Lady Vanishes* (1938), to Dr. Constance Peterson in *Spellbound* (1945), Alicia Huberman in *Notorious* (1946), Lisa Fremont in *Rear Window* (1954), Jo McKenna in *The Man Who Knew Too Much* (1956), Judy Barton in *Vertigo* (1958), Eve Kendall in *North by Northwest* (1959), and even Lila Crane in *Psycho* (1960). Like all these female characters, Charlie must make her way through a world dominated by men in search of a way to affirm her own powers but also to save the people around her at the same time. She is, as such, not only the keeper of truth but also a representative of a desire to change, to shift the stereotypical structures of a social order that wants to keep men and women on separate planes and in specified gender roles.

All this is to say that Hitchcock quite successfully brings the various components of both the film noir and melodrama together, blending these elements so that the binary dichotomy of man and woman is actually brought under a lot of pressure. What Hitchcock offers us, I would argue, is a film about the process of identification as such, or rather the process of differentiation that swallows identity as it strives to become *one* and yet is found turning on its own head, caught up in an assemblage of identifications: man that is woman that is man; film noir that is melodrama that is film noir; nocturnal that is masculine that seeks out the feminine state of the diurnal, which in turn becomes masculine in its nocturnal agency.

Hitchcock, in other words, showcases for us a filmic world that (borrowing some language from Gilles Deleuze) desires to *deterritorialize* the fixities of cinema, both in terms of the standardization of genres and of gender representations. Hitchcock's *Shadow of a Doubt* thus casts some doubtful shadows on the transhistorical feminization of the night and the nocturnalization of the feminine—a mode of identification that Bronfen carries from antiquity into the late twentieth century. Is it not possible that the twentieth century presents us with alternative social and aesthetic formulations and formations, especially as it finds itself experimenting with, and inspired by, its most popular new form of media culture: cinema?

NOCTURNALIZING THE FEMININE; FEMINIZING THE NOCTURNAL

There is a rather generalizing theoretical brushstroke being performed in Bronfen's book, which causes a significant problem for the investigation of the nocturnal. Indeed, as she moves across time connecting the representation of the night and women from one thinker or creator to the other, the nocturnal loses its temporal permutability—its *chronos*—acquiring a commonplace stability that keeps reappearing intact across various historical points, becoming, thus, nothing more than a linguistic *topos*. She offers amazingly and importantly elaborate descriptions of the appearance of the night in each work examined, but the potentially shifting nature of the night as a historically redefined concept is overshadowed by a transcendental interpretation that is performed in Bronfen's analytic operation.

In spite of this drawback in pinning down the sociohistorical permutations of the night, Bronfen does, nonetheless, offer some clarity in pointing out how the night *is* a concept around which a specific type of understanding and thinking had emerged with some repetition. As she notes, the darkness of the night works to shield us from the social demands and certainties of the day, allowing "to give ourselves over to memories or fantasies, but also to doubts, wild conjectures, and anxieties" (2013, xi). This means that the night functions in part as a shielded passage, giving us access to our hidden fantasies—our dreams and our desires. These preoccupations are presented as hidden precisely because they transgress the boundaries of the known, a sort of *known* that is connected to the delineations afforded to reality at any given time by the social norm. As such, peculiarly, our desires are covered up by the brightness of the day where the sun shines (metaphorically speaking) to disclose only that which is accepted: the law of the day, and by extension, the law of the rational and fearless man. The night, instead, presents the world to us in a new way, offering spaces that are revealed quite differently, dark alleys, secret corridors, even the simplest and most common of them all, the bed on which we recline to lose ourselves in our private thoughts and suppressed cravings before dreams and their chaos take over entirely.

At the same time, though, Bronfen points out that the night also leaves us exposed to doubts, ambivalences, new possibilities, and other foreign elements. We might be allowed a potentially revelatory access to ourselves, but we also become an open target for the workings of the maleficent nature of the night, its dark side expressed through sinister deeds and dangerous liaisons. The keyword here is the *other,* precisely because the *other* is what is presented as a connection between the subject and its opposing subjects or objects. What I mean to say here is that the night—as presented in many works discussed in Bronfen's book and especially in the examples of cosmogonies whereby the world is brought forth from the chaotic core of darkness—undoes the defining principles of the day so that the demarcated position of the self *as opposed to any other* is brought under fire as well. I would go so far as to argue that, through the powers of the night, our own self or our sense of selfhood is lost in a world of *othering*. We lose our sense of personal subjectivity, that subjectivity that has been built up for us (as Louis Althusser had so brilliantly argued [170–83]) by the regulations set forth by social appearance and naming—a process that is by nature privileged in the cold light of day. Indeed, the lost opportunity here on behalf of Bronfen's examination can be found in the potential of the night to offer a counterpart to the functions of the day not simply by existing *in opposition to* diurnal operations but by doing things in a radically different way: by breaking down any binary dichotomies that are privileged in the truth-seeking norms of the light—that is, of the Enlightenment.

The feminine is, indeed, that which is placed firmly within this nocturnal regime as Bronfen explores and describes it. As she maintains, the Enlightenment project did not simply perform an attack on the irrepresentable, the irrational, and the ungraspable. With its attack on the nocturnal regime, the rational thinker also performed an inadvertent attack on the notion of the feminine that is expressed in the form of the female figures Nyx and the Queen of the Night. Bronfen does insist on this, though her reasoning for the feminization of the nocturnal remains, in my view, loosely justified. We see this approach, though, falling within a general trend in feminist theory since the mid-1970s, which attempts to differentiate a way of thinking about gender from older arguments that were based on equality (that propose, in other words, that women are equal to, or the same as, men). This later generation of feminism seeks to emphasize women's *difference* and what the stakes of this differentiation can be.

Depending on the scholar's disciplinary specialization, the theoretical discussion of difference has been mapped onto classical myths, body parts, and reading practices. For example, drawing from Plato's discussion of *chora* as that territory peripheral to the ancient Greek polis, Julia Kristeva reintroduces the term to suggest a concept of women's time that is, in psychoanalytic terms, pre-Oedipal and presymbolic. As creative writers, Monique Wittig and Hélène Cixous both want to resist a masculinist mode of thinking and, as such, become primary discussants of a potential *écriture feminine*. While Wittig proposes a need for women's specificity to be found within themselves and outside of a comparison to men, for Cixous women are explored through their psychosexual specificity in differentiation from that of men. From a similar perspective, Luce Irigaray, going against the longstanding predominance of the phallus in Western philosophy, uses female sex organs (the clitoris, the lips of the vulva) to argue for an alternative framework of essential female difference. Moving from the French to the American context, Naomi Schor writes about "reading in detail," whereby details in art and literature and aesthetic study in general are sexually gendered. Mary Ann Doane, influenced by Irigaray's work, seeks to understand the process of identification between female spectators and female characters, proposing a form of masquerade that becomes a mode of visually performing the idea of a socially prescribed femininity. And finally Kaja Silverman theorizes about the "acoustic mirror" in film, considering the means through which the female voice in film leads us back to the maternal voice.

With this in mind, it is possible to see Bronfen's interpretation of the nocturnal as a continuation of this theoretical trajectory of difference-feminism. In her case, it is the night that becomes the metaphorical concept onto which she maps an essential femininity different from a diurnal masculinist mode of thinking. As such, the nocturnal becomes not only an interpretative object and theoretical content but also a subjective reading position that claims the forces of the night for women. Nevertheless, while the female figure of the night in Schikaneder's libretto seems to me to be a starting point for why the alternative to the enlightened subject is a feminine regime, it strikes me as problematic that there is not much analysis to ground this position substantially, especially as Bronfen continues with the nocturnal as a regime or worldview that appears again and again across hundreds of years of various Western social orders. My theoretical mind—trained as it is via a Nietzschean, Bergsonian, and Deleuzian philosophy of continuous change—finds difficulty in seeing *one type* of acting or thinking or desiring as timelessly feminine, or masculine, or akin to any other socially constructed (and thus historically divergent) gender stereotype. To be fair, it might be that Bronfen is describing what for the Enlightenment was considered feminine and masculine. As such, she might not be expressing what she herself sees as pertaining necessarily to a feminine regime. Still, as Foucault taught us ever since *The History of Sexuality,* an understanding of any type of sexuality is sociohistorically transformed and upheld. Judith Butler, in her own seminal work *Gender Trouble,* includes gender in this mode of historical permutability as well. These imperative intricacies of how one defines and approaches the feminine, long discussed by now within critical theory, seem neglected by Bronfen's discussion.

Indeed, Bronfen describes the feminine characteristics as expressed in the representation of the night as "the irrational, vengeful, romantic, magical, animalistic, musical, indeed, the spectacle of artistic expressions per se" (2013, 4). The night functions as a trope for the "unthought and the unthinkable" (19). But using the feminization of the night within a group of specifically selected philosophical and literary texts leads her to minimize the importance of the sociohistorical reality of the period under investigation. Similarly, she pays attention to the diurnal forces that aim to shed light on life through an objective distance sought out by a certain philosophical tradition. Why, though, this tradition is masculinized is a question that Bronfen does not see through to the end. The matter has, of course, been developed by numerous thinkers within the feminist tradition. Nevertheless, my concern is that Bronfen fails to acknowledge the recent history of this debate within Western scholarship where we find an array of feminist thinkers who have written quite extensively on the marginalization of women within the Enlightenment and modernity.

To begin with, in her influential essay "A Cyborg Manifesto," Donna J. Haraway turns to the dominant ocular culture that was developed within the male-centric hierarchical order of Cartesianism. As she proposes, by positioning nature and culture as *objects* of exploration, the scientific eye of the modern researcher and explorer made various subjects in society (individuals of different gender, different sexuality, different race, and so on) a form of *otherness* equal to the laws of nature, which must be analyzed in order to be tamed. Haraway finds that the main source of this objectification that leads to a hierarchical separation within social and natural worlds—one that grants the surveyor the beneficial position of master—is the very dualism "subject-object" that is maintained within a Cartesian philosophy. As the surveying, exploring, experimenting, researching, and explaining *subject* is a primarily masculine one during this time—that is, men are indeed those individuals within Western culture who are given the privilege to enter and play significant roles within the academic, scientific, and artistic circles—it is no surprise that women are found to take up the position of *object* within this structure.

The ocular also plays a central role in both Teresa de Lauretis's *Alice Doesn't* and Silverman's *On the Threshold of the Visible World*. In both cases, the cinematic camera plays an important part in positioning women as objects of the established ocularcentrism privileged within the Enlightenment and modernity. In their analysis, the camera becomes integral to the social setting of visual culture, one that favors a gazing subject objectifying those who are recorded. For de Lauretis, the position granted to women within visual culture is enforced from the outside, binding them to a mysterious world that has decided *what it is* to be a woman. Silverman looks to the apparatus as well, thinking through the relationship between the historical periods during which the various technologies were explored and invented and connecting this social order to the complexities of the psychological formations of subjectivity (and this via Lacanian psychoanalysis). Much like de Lauretis's fictional figure Alice, Silverman sees the feminine as being performed. It is a performance that has been displayed onto the female body from the ideological apparatus with which the camera (the technological invention of surveillance) has been aligned; and it is a performance that comes forth from the interplay between mirror displays and the self-reflexive search for an identity despite the dissimilarities between what one sees and how one is seen.

Central to these discussions is a sense of some form of crisis—a crisis of what feminism means, what the feminine might mean. In her own attempt at approaching this matter, Elizabeth Grosz makes the direct connection between this crisis of knowing *identity* and the overall existential anxieties that lay at the heart of the Enlightenment. As she explains, the Enlightenment was struggling to gain access to the world via a form of knowledge based on reason (25–43). It is on this epistemological directive that the feminine was being transformed, subjected to a series of erasures that would leave a stereotypically heteronormative version of womanhood available. At the same time, though, this entire project was doomed by a fundamental problematic: "the crisis of reason's *inability to rationally know itself*, to enclose and know itself from the outside: the inadequation of the subject and knowledge" (26). It is this ambiguity, this flow of continuous differentiation, this mode of knowing by transfixing, this inability to know knowledge itself—all this is what lies at the heart of the Enlightenment and, by extension, any identity politics that would include the feminine and the masculine. While Bronfen does address this crisis in terms of the Enlightenment's desire to shield the world from the nocturnal side of thought, desire, and action, she denies the same sort of crisis as central to a theory that would uphold a binary system as such: night-day, nocturnal-diurnal, feminine-masculine.

NOIR MEDITATIONS; NOCTURNAL MEDIATIONS

Night Passages is an honest and very intimate invitation for its reader, an invitation to sail adrift Bronfen's stream of theoretical reveries and interpretative meditations that seek to establish connections so-far hidden or underresearched. Overall, the author presents us with a useful addition to theoretical thinking about how darkness and femininity have been variably matched together across both media and time. Nonetheless, her desire to construct the night as a consistent theoretical concept leads her to forget the differentiation of time itself, change that feeds life into any sociohistorical structure or assemblage.

The problem here is that films that fall within the film noir tradition are cultural artifacts that fit too seamlessly into Bronfen's argument, allowing her to read in them her own theoretical nocturnalization of humanistic inquiry and artistic production as a generalized condition. Similarly, she approaches cinema as a medium in general in the same way. For instance, she explores Martin Scorsese's *Taxi Driver* (1976) as a film that exemplifies the powers of the night but one that is self-reflective as well, showcasing how cinema *is* a medium of the night. Indeed, the film is about a Vietnam veteran who, suffering from insomnia, chooses to live the life of the night; it is thus, as Bronfen maintains, a more contemporary treatment of the night similar to that of gothic literature (2013, 265). This might be so, but what does this mean for the theoretical grounding of her argument? Does a specifically identified list of cultural works justify a generalized theory of social symptomatology?

It is this analytic mode used in the book that makes me uneasy, creating some doubtful concerns with regard to the theoretical polarization between night and day, masculine and feminine. Bronfen, having chosen these very fitting—albeit accommodating—works, proceeds to state that they exemplify what is essential about cinema: the fact that it is a nocturnal medium. She writes:

> Going into the night in *Taxi Driver* is tantamount to entering a movie theater. We not only follow Scorsese's disaffected Vietnam vet as he moves even farther into the heart of the darkness of his war trauma. His psychic passages through the night also puts Scorsese's conception of film as a nocturnal medium on display, at whose navel pure nothingness appears:

> that essence of poetic imagination, that impossible vanishing of the world into pure textuality that Blanchot calls *autre nuit*. (2013, 265)

Why, though, does cinema need to be a *nocturnal* medium? Because we are in a dark cinema auditorium? Because we experience a film as if it were a dream? Because once the film ends we wake up from this event and reenter the real world where normality—the diurnal state of things—takes over again? Because we experience the cinema screen as a space for the manifestation of the dark forces of our unconscious? These propositions might indeed justify Bronfen's nocturnalization of cinema; yet she neglects to consider an idea she herself presents earlier in the book: that we carry within us the experience of the night into the day so that we are always somewhere in between the one and the other.

This is where I see the concept of the nocturnal to become most productive: that we are to be found in the interval between night and day, between truth and chaos, between desire and fear. Yet, it is an idea that is undercut by a certain identity politics that leads Bronfen to describe, or inscribe, certain characteristics for the feminine, the masculine, the night, the day, and the medium of cinema in terms of both its technology as well as its genres. In fact, cinema's more recent technological developments teach us an important lesson: by making an industry-wide shift from analog to digital technologies, cinema and the audiovisual culture to which it belongs (and that surrounds it) do not have any specific ontological truth. Instead, like theoretical concepts (nocturnal-diurnal, feminine-masculine, film noir–melodrama), cinema and media more generally continuously evolve, becoming platforms for new spectatorial experiences, creative expressions, and sociohistorical reflections that remain alive and divergent from one period to the next.[7]

It is through this very mode of differentiated theoretical conceptualization that we might acquire a more complex vision of cinema and spectatorship as such: one where any type of force (be it nocturnal or whatever else we might want to call it) is never separate from a group of other forces, all working together to engulf the viewer in a state of awakened reflectivity, reflexivity, awe, and thoughtfulness, seeing the world itself both recorded and transformed at the same time, on a screen that necessarily varies from era to era to include anything from the screen in the dark auditorium, to the brightly surrounded habitual screen of the television, to the diverse sizes and locales of computer screens, tablet devices, and phones. This is a cinema whose ontology is expressed and aestheticized as a constancy of differentiation, its own identity and that of its representations complicated in the creativity of thought, practice, experimentation, and experience.

Markos Hadjioannou is the Andrew W. Mellon Assistant Professor in the Program in Literature and the Program in the Arts of the Moving Image at Duke University. He is the author of the monograph *From Light to Byte: Toward an Ethics of Digital Cinema,* along with numerous other articles on film theory and film philosophy, as well as cinema and new media.

Notes

1. Some notable examples of this scholarship include James Naremore's *More than Night* (2008, orig. pub. 1998), Kelly Oliver and Benigno Trigo's *Noir Anxiety* (2003), Sheri Chinen Biesen's *Blackout* (2005), Jennifer Fay and Justus Nieland's *Film Noir* (2010), Jonathan Auerbach's *Dark Borders* (2011), Mark Osteen's *Nightmare Alley* (2013), and Erik Dussere's *America is Elsewhere* (2014).

2. I will explain the problem with terming film noir a "genre" per se further on in my discussion.

3. I am very fortunate to have co-taught this film at Duke University with my beloved friend and colleague Rey Chow. It is during the discussions between us and with our spring 2014 students that many of these thoughts were developed.

4. Mladen Dolar discusses the doubling effect of this formal construction at length in his essay "Hitchcock's Objects" (esp. 31–39). James McLaughlin moves the discussion further into the realm of sexuality, proposing that the sinister link between the two Charlies suggests a potentially incestuous core within the seemingly innocent family unit.

5. In her previous monograph *Home in Hollywood* (2004), Bronfen writes extensively on the importance of the home in the American melodrama, and the sense of alienation, homelessness, and of not belonging that is expressed in this genre. While she does refer to a handful of Hitchcock films, it is unfortunate that *Shadow of a Doubt* does not feature in her discussion.

6. For a brilliantly comprehensive description of the history and complexities of melodrama and women's films, see Susan Hayward's chapter on the subject in her book *Cinema Studies: The Key Concepts* (236–48).

7. This is precisely the running argument of my own monograph *From Light to Byte.*

Works Cited

Althusser, Louis. 1971. "Ideology and Ideological State Apparatuses." In *Lenin and Philosophy and Other Essays*, 127–86. Trans. Ben Brewster. New York: Monthly Review Press. (Orig. pub. 1970.)

Auerback, Jonathan. 2011. *Dark Borders: Film Noir and American Citizenship*. Durham: Duke University Press.

Biesen, Sheri Chinen. 2005. *Blackout: World War II and the Origins of Film Noir*. Baltimore: Johns Hopkins University Press.

Bronfen, Elisabeth. 2004. *Home in Hollywood: The Imaginary Geography of Cinema*. New York: Columbia University Press.

———. 2013. *Night Passages: Philosophy, Literature, and Film*. Trans. Elisabeth Bronfen and David Brenner. New York: Columbia University Press. (Orig. pub. 2008.)

Butler, Judith. 1990. *Gender Trouble: Feminism and the Subversion of Identity*. New York: Routledge.

de Lauretis, Teresa. 1984. *Alice Doesn't: Feminism, Semiotics, Cinema*. Bloomington: Indiana University Press.

Dolar, Mladen. 2010. "Hitchcock's Objects." In *Everything You Always Wanted to Know about Lacan (But Were Afraid to Ask Hitchcock)*. Ed. Slavoj Žižek, 31–46. London: Verso, 2010. (Orig. pub. 1992.)

Dussere, Erik. 2014. *America Is Elsewhere: The Noir Tradition in the Age of Consumer Culture*. New York: Oxford University Press.

Fay, Jennifer, and Justus Nieland. 2010. *Film Noir: Hard-Boiled Modernity and the Cultures of Globalization*. Routledge Film Guidebooks. Abingdon: Routledge.

Foucault, Michel. 1990. *The History of Sexuality*. Vol. 1. Trans. Robert Hurley. New York: Vintage Books. (Orig. pub. 1976.)

Grosz, Elizabeth. 1995. *Space, Time, and Perversion*. New York: Routledge.

Hadjioannou, Markos. 2012. *From Light to Byte: Toward an Ethics of Digital Cinema*. Minneapolis: University of Minnesota Press.

Haraway, Donna J. 1991. "A Cyborg Manifesto: Science, Technology, and Socialist-Feminism in the Late Twentieth Century." In *Simians, Cyborgs, and Women: The Reinvention of Nature*, 149–81. London: Free Association Books.

Hayward, Susan. 2006. *Cinema Studies: The Key Concepts*. 3rd ed. London: Routledge. (Orig. pub. 1996.)

Hitchcock, Alfred, dir. 1938. *The Lady Vanishes*. United Artists.

———. *Shadow of a Doubt*. 1943. Universal Pictures.

———. *Spellbound*. 1945. United Artists.

———. *Notorious*. 1946. RKO Radio Pictures.

———. *Rear Window*. 1954. Paramount Pictures.

———. *The Man Who Knew Too Much*. 1956. Paramount Pictures.

———. *Vertigo*. 1958. Paramount Pictures.

———. *North by Northwest*. 1959. Metro-Goldwyn-Mayer.

———. *Psycho*. 1960. Paramount Pictures.

McLaughlin, James. 2009. "All in the Family: Alfred Hitchcock's *Shadow of a Doubt.*" In *A Hitchcock Reader*. 2nd ed. Ed. Marshall Deutelbaum and Leland Poague, 145–55. Chichester: Wiley-Blackwell, 2009. (Orig. pub. 1986.)

Naremore, James. 2008. *More than Night: Film Noir in Its Contexts.* Updated and expanded ed. Berkeley: University of California Press. (Orig. pub. 1998.)

Oliver, Kelly, and Benigno Trigo. 2003. *Noir Anxiety.* Minneapolis: University of Minnesota Press.

Osteen, Mark. 2013. *Nightmare Alley: Film Noir and the American Dream.* Baltimore: Johns Hopkins University Press.

Scorsese, Martin, dir. 1976. *Taxi Driver.* Columbia Pictures.

Siegel, Don, dir. 1956. *Invasion of the Body Snatchers.* Allied Artists Pictures.

Silver, Alain, and Elizabeth Ward, eds. 1979. *Film Noir: An Encyclopedic Reference to the American Style.* Woodstock, N.Y.: Overlook Press.

Silverman, Kaja. 1996. *The Threshold of the Visible World.* New York: Routledge.

Wilder, Billy, dir. 1944. *Double Indemnity.* Paramount Pictures.

THE PERILS OF COMPARISON IN SUBALTERN STUDIES AND ITS CRITIQUE

POSTCOLONIAL THEORY AND THE SPECTER OF CAPITAL
BY VIVEK CHIBBER
Verso, 2013

Travis Workman

In the three years since the publication of Vivek Chibber's *Postcolonial Theory and the Specter of Capital,* a number of responses and reviews have appeared, some from scholars in subaltern studies and postcolonial theory whom Chibber criticizes and others from more sympathetic readers and interlocutors (Brennan; Chatterjee; Spivak 2014). Although this essay is a review of Chibber's book, the debates that emerged around the text are perhaps more revealing of contemporary problems in Marxism and postcolonial theory, because they speak to certain impasses in both fields of inquiry. From the perspective of Chibber, and I suspect many who support his argument, these debates are between, on the one hand, a postcolonial studies field that has left behind its initial interest in Marxism and become mired in poststructuralist platitudes about the virtue of fragmentation and the danger of totalizing theories, and, on the other hand, a Marxist approach that sees fragments and difference—as well as identities other than the proletariat and the intellectual vanguard—as having a conciliatory relationship with the social totality constituted by capital. For Chibber, the situation demands a return to Enlightenment universals and reason as the necessary epistemological bases for a critique of capitalism and the potential liberation from its exploitation. Chibber's critics, on the other hand, point to his reduction of Marxism to a positivist sociology, the basing of his critiques of subaltern studies almost solely in a reading of the English and French Revolutions, and his tendency to caricature the work of esteemed intellectuals like Ranajit Guha, Partha Chatterjee, and Dipesh Chakrabarty with accusations of essentialism, irrationality, and even Orientalism.

The unfortunate terms of this debate, mostly established by Chibber's text, make Marxism and postcolonial theory appear at odds by way of a set of old colonial binaries: rational vs. irrational, Europe vs. Asia, universalism vs. particularism, concepts vs. identity, Enlightenment vs. premodern ontology, and so on. While we might consider the reemergence of these binaries as a reflection of two strains of Marxist thinking, one positivist and the other humanist and interpretive (this is Timothy Brennan's assertion), I will approach them rather through the problem and dialectics of historical, political, and cultural comparison. I do so not to highlight differences between European and Asian capitalism or modernity but rather to think critically about the confluence of Enlightenment universalism and Marxism asserted by Chibber without relying, as subaltern studies does, on the categories of the West and the East, as though these terms can mark an essential cultural, social, or historical difference.

Chibber arrives at his reading of postcolonial theory through a number of general and legitimate concerns about postcolonial theory. Postcolonial theory often forgoes a critique of contemporary capitalism for the sake of an analysis of oppression focused on colonial dynamics, even though it is largely practiced in the academies of the former and current imperialist countries. When postcolonialism is understood too chronologically, as the "after" of colonialism, colonialism itself loses its historical specificity and the analysis of postcolonial culture can become tacitly complicit with the imperial political formations that have superseded colonialism. The primary problem that postcolonial theory needs to confront is the relationship between its objects of study and the form of capitalism in the historical present.

For Chibber, responding to these concerns requires confronting the dominant academic fashions in which postcolonial theory partakes and asserting the need to return to Marxian sociological analysis. Therefore, *Postcolonial Theory* begins with a familiar invective against contemporary philosophy and theory, particularly in the humanities. The primary targets are postcolonial theory and poststructuralism. Despite the capacity for the academic marketplace to subject all manner of thought, including Marxism, to the rule of the commodity form, postcolonial theory and poststructuralism have been brought to task more than other humanities and social science theories for their compatibility with capitalism's logic of assimilation through differentiation. By now these kinds of arguments against the opacity and meaninglessness of contemporary cultural theory feel journalistic, not to say cliché, and it would be a shame if the only way of writing available to thought were Chibber's brand of social science. The choice presented, Marxism vs. poststructuralist theory, seems unnecessarily simplistic, as much more sophisticated means have been developed to articulate and to conceptualize the intersection of the universal and the particular in modernity (from theories of translation to geographic Marxism). In relation to the problem of "universality," instead of grasping for Enlightenment universals in the most generic sense of the term, one could begin, among other places, with Etienne Balibar's distinction between real, fictive, and ideal universality, in order to think toward universality without reifying it by way of positivism (Balibar). Or if one prefers, what about the work on Marx's notion of "general intellect" and the turn to theories of generality that do not seek universalization (Virno)? In light of recent intellectual history, the demand that *Postcolonial Theory* makes on the reader to choose between Derrida and sociology feels false.

I am sympathetic with certain aspects of Chibber's project, because I too think that the general lack of interest in Marxist categories and modes of analysis has contributed to the banality and loss of critical potential in postcolonial studies. Nonetheless, in order to demolish what he sees as the radical chic of postcolonial theory, Chibber has chosen to attack some of the more historically grounded and penetrating works of social theory produced within postcolonial theory, the work of the subaltern studies group. I do not agree with all of the positions taken in the work of the subaltern studies group, and I am not a scholar of South Asian history in any case. However, considering subaltern studies' relationship with the rest of postcolonial theory and the North American academy at large, it is not the best or most symptomatic example of the academic fashions that Chibber inveighs against. Much of the book bends the arguments of the subaltern studies group in order to make them conform to the object that he needs for his own destructive project, which is a faulty empirical social science at the foundation of all of the cultural, literary, and historical work done in the name of postcolonial theory in the last thirty years. This positivist attempt to take the rug out from under theory by pointing to the faulty empirical base inevitably relies on caricature and does not explain culturally and historically why postcolonial theory has persisted in late capitalism despite its so-called "mistakes." In this respect, older texts on postcolonial studies by Arif Dirlik, Benita Parry, and Harry Harootunian remain more convincing because they do not simply show the logical or empirical uncertainty of a few claims of one branch of postcolonial studies but outline the late capitalist and post–Cold War conditions within which postcolonial theory thrives and reproduces itself as a form of knowledge (Dirlik; Harootunian; Parry). Historicizing postcolonial theory in our present requires some mode of immanent textual analysis. Chibber's claim that only in subaltern studies do we find anything conceptually and empirically substantial to evaluate in postcolonial theory says more about his unwillingness to work through arguments in the theoretical humanities than to the true exemplarity of the group.

In any case, by entering into the debates around Chibber's book it becomes clear that the boundary between postcolonial studies and Marxism is much more porous than the above distinctions between dialectic totality and the philosophies of difference would suggest. In Gayatri Spivak's review of the book and Partha Chatterjee's oral response to it, for example, it is apparent that despite Chibber's effort to portray postcolonial theory as inherently and broadly anti-Marxist, the primary problems understood and addressed by both sides of the debate are still unresolved problems *within* Marxism: the "transition" from feudalism to capitalism in various parts of the world, the relationship between capitalism and precapitalist modes of production, the colonial state in the era of imperialism, the role of Reason in the spread of capitalism and in its critique, the political relationship between the industrial proletariat and other exploited classes (particularly peasants), real versus formal subsumption, the significance or insignificance of culture in the reproduction of capital, the effects of gender and race on the modes of capitalist exploitation, the status of abstract labor and the labor theory of value, and so on. Chibber thinks that these problems can be worked through by way of positivist social science research, by establishing a single factual record of the history of capitalism and analyzing political and economic behaviors with categories like physical well-being, choices, and interests (both individual and collective). On the other hand, subaltern studies (which Chibber treats as a synecdoche for postcolonial theory) would tend to see this type of sociological analysis as part of the colonial legacy of capitalism, from the colonial versions of utilitarian thought in nineteenth-century India, to the modernizing ethos of many Indian nationalists, to modernization theory and eventually neoliberalism.

For Chibber, this critique amounts to an abandonment of reason and Enlightenment universals, but his version of this real disagreement about methodology is a little misleading. According to subaltern studies, the colonial legacy of the empirical human sciences and their connection with the logic of capitalism does not demand a total abandonment of reason but a delinking of reason from its identity with the instrumentality of capitalism, the colonial state, and the developmental postcolonial state. Postcolonial theory, and particularly subaltern studies, does not discard reason tout court. In the variants of postcolonial theory that are not totally immersed in culturalism, the tendency is rather to ask whether a future society might overcome what Chatterjee refers to as "the cunning of reason" or the "identity of Reason and capital," particularly in those regions of the world and among those groups of people that were most oppressively rendered the anthropological objects of Enlightenment thought (Chatterjee, 170). Chibber dismisses these lines of Chatterjee's concerning the identity of reason and capital at the end of *Nationalist Thought and the Colonial World,* and it is true that Chatterjee could have explored this connection to capital with more attention to political economy in the main body of the text. However, Chibber tries so much to create an image of an excessively romantic and identity-driven subaltern studies critiquing Enlightenment in every form that he is obligated by this point in his own reading to dismiss Chatterjee's discussion of capital as an internal inconsistency and an apology that comes too late.

While Chatterjee's reading of nationalism and his representation of peasant consciousness may in the end have significant limitations, portraying him as an anti-Enlightenment Orientalist confuses the diagnostic aspects of Chatterjee's work with a prescription for an antimodern political project (although one could ask whether or not socialism should not be antimodern in many ways). According to Chibber, Chatterjee "carefully levels his main criticism against the idea of modernization itself," and this particular reading of the identity of reason and capital can only be a reactionary and Orientalist turn away from a radical Enlightenment that is necessary for Marxism as a political and epistemological project. However, in the sample of subaltern studies texts that Chibber analyzes as postcolonial theory's social theory—mainly Ranajit Guha's *Dominance without Hegemony*, Chatterjee's *Nationalist Thought*, and Dipesh Chakrabarty's *Provincializing Europe*—varied discussions of the problem of reason and conceptualization appear and often through a much subtler and immanent critique than Chibber's accusations of anti-Enlightenment would suggest. Chakrabarty's questionable Heideggerian celebration of peasant consciousness notwithstanding, these intellectuals' reflections on the relation—which is perhaps a better term than "identity"—between reason, capitalism, and colonialism do not add up to a clearly antimodern and anti-Marxist position.

For example, if one reads Chatterjee's critique of the identity of reason and capital in *Nationalist Thought* alongside Frankfurt school texts on instrumental reason or the dialectic of Enlightenment, one finds significant homologies. As both Theodor Adorno and Chatterjee are equally aware, nationalism, romanticism, irrationality, racism, and even fascist politics are not the obverse of Enlightenment reason, as Chibber would like to claim in an overly neat separation. In modernity Enlightenment universals are both a potential means of liberation and a means of reification and the legitimation of exploitation, or worse. The historical exploration of the deep relationship between the dialectic of Enlightenment and imperial and colonial projects is probably the most important contribution postcolonial theory has made to the humanities and social sciences, and it should not be cast aside so efficiently.

Subaltern studies texts and much of postcolonial theory offer an *internal* critique of both Enlightenment and Marxism. How would Chibber's version of radical Enlightenment differ from such critique? This is where he turns to positivist social scientific categories and modes of analysis in the Anglo-American tradition, attempting to locate the material basis for all social actions in the struggle for self-preservation and class interests. While I agree that attention to these basic material factors in history is lacking in much contemporary work in social theory, his approach leaves a number of phenomena unexplained, phenomena that subaltern studies and postcolonial theory are rightfully interested in exploring. These would include the colonial racism of the metropolitan working class and settler colonials, the role of religion and culture in political action, ideology's capacity to make subjects act against their own self-interest or class interests, the gendering of class, and the ways that "physical well-being" becomes biopolitical when the needs of some are pitted against the existence of others. In the better postcolonial theory, exploring these issues is not a matter of giving up on any class analysis but rather of tracing the intersections of class with these other factors in the social process of imperialism, particularly the displacements and modes of identification that exceed the pursuit of interests and the effects of direct state repression.

While other avenues of postcolonial theory may be much more dismissive of Marxist categories, subaltern studies, even in its most culturalist moments, remains engaged with Marx, while also exploring relationships between Marx's nineteenth-century mode of analysis and the history of imperialism and colonialism. In this respect, Chibber has chosen a useful target, because he purports to find the origins of most of the problems of postcolonial theory in the faults of the social scientific articulation closest to his own methodology. However, this also leads him to make some questionable statements, such as the effects he attributes to Guha's incorrect understanding of the history of the English and French Revolutions, an understanding taken directly from Marx's own "Whig" interpretation of these revolutions as bourgeois, antifeudal, and effecting the economic and political hegemony of the bourgeois state. According to Chibber, Guha takes up the Conventional Story that the English and French Revolutions were bourgeois revolutions that led to the establishment of bourgeois political and cultural hegemony over the working class. Through the use of this counterfactual, Guha is able to present the case that the Indian bourgeois nationalists, and others in the "East," obtained the power to dominate without the kind of political hegemony gained by the English and French bourgeoisies. Chibber states that Guha gives no attention to later developments in Marxist histories of these European revolutions, and therefore in his claim for colonial difference regarding the hegemony of the bourgeoisie we can find the origins of postcolonial theory's essentialism (not only of its insistence that the form of capitalism in the colonies is somewhat different from the form of capitalism in the metropole, but to fundamental cultural and social differences between West and East).

Chibber attacks Guha for basically two quotations from Marx on the English and French Revolutions. In the three-chapter response to Guha's two quotations, Chibber argues that he gets the European case wrong but the Indian one right and that the bourgeoisie was not and is not interested in establishing a consensual order. Chibber's claim goes against most accepted understandings of the power of the nation-state and liberal ideology, particularly if we look past the seventeenth and eighteenth centuries to the history of imperialism and to Guha's contemporary moment. Granted there may be an anachronous aspect to Guha's placing of the construction of a consensual liberal order in the seventeenth and eighteenth centuries. However, is Chibber serious when he claims that the bourgeoisie in the so-called West has never had any interest in creating a consensual order? If the bourgeoisie is not interested in a consensual order then how and why do Chibber's vaunted Enlightenment universals exist in the first place? Or did the bourgeoisie have no part in developing the worldviews that facilitate the integration of the working class into the late capitalist nation-state, regional economy, or neoliberal international community? Chibber's reading of these European revolutions, while reflecting the most current scholarship on the transition from feudalism to capitalism in England and France, still appears pedantic in comparison to Guha's treatment of the cultures and economy of colonial and postcolonial India.

The strategy of criticizing Guha's understanding of the French and English Revolutions also does not provide a particularly pene-trating examination of the essentialism that does surface problemati-cally in postcolonial theory and subaltern studies. The fact that both Guha and Chibber refer, without pause, to the metropole as the "West" and the colony as the "East," as if these were coherent cultural or geo-graphic entities, suggests the degree to which getting the history of European revolutions correct still leaves a number of questionable cul-tural and social categories in place. Both could take notice that there are many advanced capitalist countries outside of the putative West and that the putative East is not the only place where rural peasant life persists. Without assuming an essential difference between the form of capitalism in the metropole and the colony, a difference that I agree is overstated in subaltern studies texts, we are still left with the question of how to analyze and employ the discursive categories (not the factual reality) of West and East within a coeval modernity whose economic and political foundation is the imperialist expansion of capitalism. It is my suspicion that this task cannot be undertaken properly either through subaltern studies' positing of the colony as the place of real epistemological and economic limits to the expansion of capitalism (here I agree with aspects of Chibber's criticism) or through Chibber's insistence that a correct understanding of the emergence of capitalism in England and France is the only necessary foundation from which to correctly understand its nineteenth- and twentieth-century imperialist iterations.

Rather than spending so many pages taking Guha to task for briefly quoting Marx on England and France, it would have been more useful to explain why and how Guha mistakenly articulates his political economic theory through the West and East binary. However, this would require a discursive analysis, not just fact-hunting. In any case, more significant than Guha's discussion of the failure of the Indian bourgeoisie to manufacture hegemony, which does establish European capitalism as a false norm and counterfactual, are the insights he makes into problems within Marxism in an analysis of its imperialist stage, problems that a more accurate history of the English and French Revolutions are very unlikely to resolve. Spivak has pointed out some of these in her review of Chibber's book and they include, but are not limited to, the gendered division of labor (especially the distinction between waged and unwaged labor), the international division of labor, uneven geographic distribution of value, the persistence of slavery in the capitalist era, and the real, global existence of subaltern classes that do not belong properly to the industrial or postindustrial proletariat (Spivak 2014). Although Chibber argues that Guha is not really a Marxist, Guha's text contains analyses of these problems within Marxism while Chibber passes over them in favor of a return to the rudiments of the labor theory of value.

Chibber wishes to leave out the possibility of any form of labor that is not abstract labor, because he assumes that the methods of quantifying value created by capitalism can provide an adequate picture of exploitation; unfortunately for this theory, not all labor is wage labor, particularly in societies such as colonial and postcolonial India. Guha's statements about domestic servants and other nonwage workers approaches the question from a more materialist position informed by Marxist feminism rather than assuming that the introduction of "market dependence" necessarily means that all labor becomes quantifiable abstract labor. Although I think that Chakrabarty's distinction between History 1 (abstract labor) and History 2 (precapitalist cultural consciousness and practice) is not a particularly useful way of dividing the analysis of history, Chibber can only claim later in the book that History 2 is subsumable into History 1 by assuming that all labor is abstract labor and that behind every decision to labor there is the pursuit of physical well-being, individual interests, and class interests. Chibber's framework ignores the gendered dimension of reproduction and of unwaged household labor by assuming that only labor that is quantified in the capitalist labor market is the proper object of Marxist analysis. Guha's use of the term "subaltern" emerged precisely in his attempt to see past the way that Marxism had limited the category of worker to the industrial proletariat. "Working class" cannot stand in for all exploited classes with no attention to the uneven politics and economy of value and their relation to gender, social space, race, and a number of other factors.

The fallacy of subsuming all work into a homogeneous working class also pertains to the status of the peasantry. When Chibber impugns subaltern studies for not questioning why the working class of India did not revolt in the manner of the Chinese or Vietnamese working class—completely ignoring, through the very term "working class," the rural, antifeudal, and indeed subaltern character of those communist revolutions—it becomes apparent that despite its repetition of historicist and culturalist categories such as the West–East binary, subaltern studies continues to have something to teach metropolitan Marxism about the imperialist stage of capitalism, anticolonial revolutions, and social class. One could turn Chibber's charge against Guha back against him: haven't the distinct characteristics of such rural communist revolutions been analyzed historically in sufficient detail for Chibber to make *them* the comparative reference, and with a more complex understanding of social class than is offered by analyses of seventeenth- and eighteenth-century England and France?

In this respect, considering the political and economic conditions of many colonial and postcolonial countries, it should not be surprising that subaltern studies and postcolonial theory have not tended to turn to England or France but to Marx's Germany or Gramsci's Italy when in need of a comparative European reference. Chibber ignores the fact that in the quotation Guha uses Marx discusses England and France in order to contrast them with Germany during the same period, which Guha finds apt for India because it points to the persistence of precapitalist social relations well into the nineteenth century despite integration into the world market. This does not contradict Chibber's own discussion of England and France, which were different precisely because their agricultural production had already come under the sway of capitalism. It does, however, beg the question of what Chibber has to say about Marx's Germany or Gramsci's Italy, since they are the more significant comparative references for subaltern studies. He criticizes Chatterjee's application of the Gramscian notion of "passive revolution" to India but then turns to England and France rather than to Italy to prove his case. This approach of attacking the false counterfactual rather than the apt comparison leads to many more ahistorical comparisons than those that subaltern studies draws between India, Germany, and Italy, whatever the final verdict on the theory of "passive revolution" might be.

Another issue in relation to Germany is that before he was a scientific socialist Marx was a powerful critic of the seductiveness of political and philosophical idealism in semifeudal societies. Of course he arrived at materialism through a critical reading of German idealism, which is precisely the stakes in the subaltern studies group's interpretations of the particularities of bourgeois nationalism in India and the bourgeoisie's incomplete and fraught effort to nationalize the peasantry by various means. The power of philosophical idealism has deep repercussions for other histories, including my areas of the Japanese empire and colonial Korea. Chibber criticizes the focus that Guha puts on the agency of the bourgeoisie, but to claim that there is no place for such critique in Marxism in tantamount to claiming that "The German Ideology" need not have been written. In a funny quip directed at Proudhon, Marx states, "If the Englishman transforms men into hats, the German transforms hats into ideas" (87). It seems that Chibber has no interest in the second half of this statement, which speaks to the legacy of German idealism, the way that material problems of economy and politics were transformed into spiritual problems through philosophical and nationalist idealism in much of the colonial world, in addition to fascist Germany, Italy, and Japan. Pheng Cheah recognizes the power of German idealism, organic notions of social totality, and communalism in *Spectral Nationality*; Spivak provides a postcolonial reading of Kant, Hegel, and Marx in *The Critique of Postcolonial Reason* because of Germany's liminal place in imperialist Europe; and more conventional Marxist texts such as Perry Anderson's *The Indian Ideology* draw direct connections between the Indian bourgeoisie criticized by Guha and German idealism as Marx interpreted it. As far as I can tell, the fact that Chibber circumvents this line of intellectual history, as well as Gramsci, in order to harp on the correct history of the English and French Revolutions speaks more to his own formation in Anglo-American social science than necessarily to the fallacies of the comparisons that appear in subaltern studies works. In contrast to the false counterfactuals that Chibber attacks, these comparisons between India, Germany, and Italy in subaltern studies and postcolonial theory also significantly disrupt the West and East binary, and charges of Orientalism, by reestablishing a common ground for comparison with Europe.

The problem of philosophical idealism and its real historical effects pertains to the issues of hegemony and capital's universalizing tendency. Beginning with Guha, Chibber argues that subaltern studies falsely assumes that the bourgeoisie seeks hegemony and that capital's universalizing tendency finds a true limit in the colony (hence the failure of the Indian bourgeoisie). However, according to my reading, Guha is perfectly aware that the Indian economy was integrated into the world market through colonialism and argues only that the capitalist mode of production had not achieved full universalization (one could say that formal subsumption had taken place, but not real subsumption—a distinction that might clarify some of the theoretical quandaries in the debate). As for what Guha states about hegemony, he discusses universalization at the level of politics and culture, which are of course related to but not to be confused with economy. Chibber takes subaltern studies to task for locating the universalizing tendency of capitalism in the establishment of a liberal political order rather than in market dependence, but clearly Guha has both the economic and the political registers in mind when he states that the universalizing tendency of capital derives from the self-expansion of capital. Its function is to create a world market, subjugate all antecedent modes of production, and replace all jural and institutional concomitants of such modes and generally the entire edifice of precapitalist cultures by laws, institutions, values, and other elements of a culture appropriate to bourgeois rule. (Guha, 13–14)

It could be that such a statement puts too much emphasis on political hegemony and not enough on the laws of the capitalist market, but clearly a reference to both is intended. Even when capitalism is entirely pervasive under real subsumption, the political and economic project of capitalism fails in various minute aspects of social life as well as through the material and political limits to the realization of capital, whether in Europe or in Asia. Chibber confuses the universalizing *tendency* of capital with the complete integration of social life under rules dictated by market dependence, rules that can only be studied with Enlightenment universals such as choices and interests, which are produced by the very economic system that they are supposed to understand. There is a tautological dimension to his reading of universality that leads him to treat Guha's positing of the colony as a limit to capitalism in starker terms than Guha himself, who nowhere claims, as far as I am aware, that India somehow existed outside of the world market. If Guha referred to the Indian economy with the phrase "combined and uneven development" rather than describing the cultural and social complexities underlying this phrase, he may have escaped criticism.

Guha's point seems to be rather that an economic integration and building of a consensual order is particularly difficult in India and for the Indian bourgeoisie because of the existence in the 1950s and 1960s of a large rural population that no longer existed in England and France. Therefore, the degree of ideological integration of national populations at particularly moments in history is a significant problem to address in trying to assess the existence or nonexistence of a plan for consensual order. If capitalism is only a system of domination and does not also require cultural and political hegemony then one is hard-pressed to explain how nationalist ideology functioned in imperialist projects to integrate the European and American working classes in the twentieth century. I understand that Chibber wants to give the working class agency over its own political achievements, but only through a concept such as hegemony can one explain the other side of state repression, the political and discursive integration of labor unions and anticapitalist organizations into capitalism and the liberal political order. Ignoring the effort to create ideological consensus also leaves us no way to examine the nationalization of the metropolitan working class through war. It is not sociologically incorrect to state that the same degree of cultural and political integration into capitalism—including international institutions and the nation-state—did not exist in postcolonial India.

The lack of the existence of such a consensual liberal order in India can perhaps be explained in part by the lack of strong peasant-labor organizations, an important shift of emphasis that Chibber makes in his account. But the more significant difference is that a peasant class existed in India at all in the periods under analysis. Chatterjee states in his oral response to Chibber that by the East Guha actually meant the present-day peasants of the Global South. This is perhaps a retrospective insight, but nonetheless an important explanation for the terminological displacement of the peasant into the category of the East, which Chibber seems willing to grapple with only through comparison with the origin, or those countries whose peasantry has been gone for at least a century (England and France).

Chibber's discussion skirts the issue of the contemporary existence of peasants and other subaltern classes, incorporating them into a homogeneous notion of the "working class." And yet in *Habitations of Modernity,* Dipesh Chakrabarty writes, "It can be seen in retrospect that *Subaltern Studies* was a democratic project meant to produce a genealogy of the peasant as citizen in contemporary political modernity" (Chakrabarty 2002, 12). The idea and the reality that a peasant can also become a citizen points to how in modernity class categories do not refer to static states of being but rather modes of becoming. In any case, Chakrabarty makes it clear that the subaltern studies project is concerned with the distinction between West and East only insofar as this binary registers the difference between societies in which peasants no longer exist and societies in which they still do. Therefore, when Chibber uses Eugen Weber's narrative in *Peasants into Frenchmen: The Modernization of Rural France (1870–1914)* in order to criticize Guha's quotation of Marx on the English and French revolutions, stating that the establishment of bourgeois hegemony happened much later than the seventeenth and eighteenth centuries, he still has not addressed

Chakrabarty's simple point that the same process of primitive accumulation and the nationalization of the peasantry is not yet complete in India. This fact explains why a rural political movement like the Naxalites was still possible in India when it was unimaginable in France. While I am not in the position to judge the historical record in much detail, I am left wondering how Chibber can use Weber's book as proof that Guha fatefully misreads the English and French Revolutions, at the same time as Chakrabarty uses the same text to define the specific object of subaltern studies within Marxist historiography—those societies where the peasantry persists as a political subject and a political agent (Chakrabarty 2002, 15).

Add to such confusion a statement such as Chatterjee's that Guha, in quoting Marx on the English and French Revolutions, was not concerned with the English bourgeoisie of the seventeenth century or the French bourgeoisie of the eighteenth century but rather with those countries in the 1950s, and it becomes more and more difficult to tell what the period of capitalism under discussion might be or how to work through the layers of comparison. We are left, again, and despite Said's analysis, with two ahistorical and eternal categories, the West and the East, which can either be compared or not compared, and it becomes possible for Chibber to accuse subaltern studies of Orientalism and assert the need to return to Enlightenment universals. The irony is that the idea of the East, the anthropological construction of the non-West, and the racial knowledge that established the modern West and East binary are a few of these Enlightenment universals to which no one should like to return.

As should be obvious by now, *Postcolonial Theory and the Specter of Capital* and the debates that emerged around it are in large part concerned with the politics of comparison. In Chibber's ideal world, comparison is enabled by the fact that the same laws and rules of capital and capitalism are applicable in any context. And yet in order to establish this homogeneous field of interpretation in which all social action is subsumable into social science, he has to reestablish the universality of the first instance, as if the economic foundations of the social process of primitive accumulation means that this process and its effects on intellectual, cultural, and political history will look the same every time. In pointing out the way that Marxism at some point shifts from an analysis of objective economic processes to such prescriptive and normative paradigms, with a subjective center in the so-called West, postcolonial theory has posed some legitimate questions to Marxism. On the other hand, when the mode of comparison in some subaltern studies and postcolonial theory denies the power of global capitalism to uproot and transform every cultural and social formation in the world for the purposes of extracting value, this certainly leads to another kind of blindness. As the peasant classes of the world gradually disappear and industrial and postindustrial capitalism penetrates the furthest reaches of human societies, a scientific rendering of this social totality is called for, and perhaps more urgently needed than reflections on the peasant revolts of the past. However, I remain unconvinced that Chibber's replacement of the concepts of hegemony and culture with interests and physical well-being is up to this task. Considering the limited spatial and temporal orientations of the Enlightenment, I also think that questioning Enlightenment universals would have to be a significant part of the development of such a science. Trying to come to grips with the planetary scale requires new ways of connecting worlds, new directions for comparison that unmake or even forget to mention the West and the East. In this respect, the worlds that subaltern studies attempted to describe may be disappearing, but that does not mean that such worlds did not exist or do not continue to impact the present as another kind of specter.

Travis Workman is associate professor in the Department of Asian Languages and Literatures at the University of Minnesota. He is the author of *Imperial Genus: The Formation and Limits of the Human in Modern Korea and Japan* (2016).

Works Cited

Anderson, Perry. 2013. *The Indian Ideology*. London: Verso.

Balibar, Etienne. 2012. "Ambiguous Universality." In *Politics and the Other Scene*, 146–76. London: Verso.

Brennan, Timothy. 2014. "Subaltern Stakes." *New Left Review* 89 (Sept/Oct): 67–87.

Chakrabarty, Dipesh. 2000. *Provincializing Europe: Postcolonial Theory and Historical Difference*. Princeton: Princeton University Press.

———. 2002. *Habitations of Modernity: Essays in the Wake of Subaltern Studies*. Chicago: University of Chicago Press.

Chatterjee, Partha. 1999. *Nationalist Thought and the Colonial World*. In *The Partha Chatterjee Omnibu*. London: Oxford University Press.

Cheah, Pheng. 2003. *Spectral Nationality: Passages of Freedom from Kant to Postcolonial Literatures of Liberation*. New York: Columbia University Press.

Chibber, Vivek. 2013. *Postcolonial Theory and the Specter of Capital*. London: Verso.

"Debate: Marxism and the Legacy of Subaltern Studies—Historical Materialism NY 2013." 2013. http://www.youtube.com/watch?v=xbM8HJrxSJ4.

Dirlik, Arif. 1998. *The Postcolonial Aura: Third World Criticism in the Age of Global Capitalism*. Boulder, Colo.: Westview Press.

Guha, Ranajit. 1998. *Dominance without Hegemony: History and Power in Colonial India*. Cambridge, Mass.: Harvard University Press.

Harootunian, Harry. 2002. "Postcoloniality's Unconscious / Area Studies' Desire." In *Learning Places: The Afterlives of Area Studies*, 150–74. Durham: Duke University Press.

Marx, Karl. 1956. *The Poverty of Philosophy*. London: Lawrence.

———. 1974. *The German Ideology*. Ed. C. J. Arthur. London: Lawrence and Wishart.

Parry, Benita. 2002. "Signs of Our Times: A Discussion of Homi Bhabha's *The Location of Culture*." In *Learning Places: The Afterlives of Area Studies*, 119–49. Durham: Duke University Press.

Spivak, Gayatri Chakravorty. 1999. *A Critique of Postcolonial Reason: Toward a History of the Vanishing Present*. Cambridge, Mass.: Harvard University Press.

———. 2014. Review of *Postcolonial Theory and the Specter of Capital*, by Vivek Chibber. *Cambridge Review of International Affairs* 27, no. 1: 184–98.

Virno, Paolo. 2004. *A Grammar of the Multitude: For an Analysis of Contemporary Forms of Life*. Trans. Isabella Bertoletti. Los Angeles: Semiotext(e).

BOOK REVIEWS

Cultural Critique's commitment to cultural and intellectual debate and discussion is bolstered by the regular inclusion of reviews of both new and not-so-new books. Generally, books reviewed will have appeared within the past three years, although reviews of older books that are emerging or reemerging in intellectual debates are also welcome. As an academic publication, *Cultural Critique* sees itself as having a responsibility to devote space to authors whose work may not be otherwise reviewed. For *Cultural Critique*'s special issues, book reviews should share the issue's thematic focus. *Cultural Critique*'s book review editors solicit writers, books, and ideas for future contributions to this section of the journal. Please contact the book review editors at cultcrit@umn. edu or *Cultural Critique*, Department of Cultural Studies and Comparative Literature, 216 Pillsbury Drive S.E., 235 Nicholson Hall, University of Minnesota, Minneapolis, MN 55455-0229.

THE "KNOW-SHOW" FUNCTION AND THE USES OF EVIDENCE

PAPER KNOWLEDGE: TOWARD A MEDIA HISTORY OF DOCUMENTS
BY LISA GITELMAN
Duke University Press, 2014

Benedict Stork

For media historian Lisa Gitelman, documents are an especially attractive category—or, as she prefers, genre—for engaging the history of technological reproduction, media culture, and the relationship between producers and consumers of "paper knowledge." Spurred on by the conviction that the significance of documents (unlike, for instance, novels or political speeches) is inseparable from their material form, *Paper Knowledge* argues that this "genre" of printed material offers Janus-faced access to the specificity of both their technological production and the social world of their consumers and producers. As its title suggests, the text delimits documents as generally paper, or paper-like, reproducible objects exhibiting a relation with one or more institutions, which is manifest in both their physicality and their "content." In addition, documents are "material objects intended as evidence and processed or framed . . . as such"; that is, documents are fodder for arguments (Gitelman, 2). This last aspect undergirds the body of Professor Gitelman's analysis, even if it remains largely subsumed within the particular case studies. Indeed, the tension between argument and evidence is symptomatic of the book's critical bind insofar as the insistence on a certain sort of evidence—archival, material, and in some form or other, rarefied—obscures what argument it is meant to serve, as though the argument is inherent to the document.

If the characterization of documents established at the start appears at once very broad (made of paper or resembling paper, institutional in some form, etc.) and oddly restrictive (words and printed lines, but not photographic images), this is a product of the book's far-reaching ambitions and insistence on specificity. *Paper Knowledge*, explicitly or implicitly, has at least three goals: to dispute the one-size-fits-all approach to "print culture" that reduces all printed material to Gutenberg's press, to question the proclaimed break with materiality and paper in the study of "new media," and to provide a particular historical account of the document via particular print technologies. This last effort is expected to carry the weight of the others through its employment of a specific sort of evidence capable of at once disrupting the hegemonic "Gutenberg" narrative and illustrating the continuous and prefigurative role of paper documents in digital media. The challenge of this task is signaled by the book's subtitle, "Toward a Media History of Documents," which both identifies the type of history (media history) employed and proclaims its unfinished and speculative status (toward). While there is a productive dimension to this split between the definite and speculative in the subtitle—which, to some extent, catalyzes the book's movement from job printing to the *.pdf digital format—the argument necessitated by this divide is largely obscured by the narrative of each media instance. Throughout, the reader may wonder what exactly is the relationship between the concrete, if incomplete, chronicle of the social life of documents (and the media that generate them) and the suggestive hints at more pointed analyses critically situating the document as an essential genre of modernity and what Gitelman calls "managerial capital."

At the heart of *Paper Knowledge*'s conception of the document is what Gitelman calls the "know-show function," writing on the introduction's first page,

> Documents help define and are mutually defined by the know-show function, since documenting is an epistemic practice: the kind of knowing that is all wrapped up with showing, and showing wrapped up with knowing. Documents are epistemic objects; they are the recognizable sites and subjects of interpretation across the disciplines and beyond, evidential structures in the long human history of clues. (1)

This is as direct a definition of the "know-show function" as Gitelman offers, but based on its use in the subsequent treatment of documents, despite a lack of direct elaboration, the relation between knowing and showing is supposedly determined by the combination of the document's specific materiality and the use to which it is put. Whatever knowledge a document grants its user/interpreter is inseparable from its material form and the social practices it engenders and partakes in. What the document "shows" is never a simple content but an instantiation of the knowledge gleaned from it in particular encounters and arguments. Foregrounding this aspect of documents, as the book's immediate invocation of the "know-show function" does, amounts to emphasizing documents' contested status, presumably to unsettle the two disciplinary formations *Paper Knowledge* challenges. In terms of "print culture," documents (and their knowing-showing) disrupt the homogenization of "print" by demanding that the scope of the "textual economy" move beyond Gutenberg's letter press (and the latent technological determinism associated with it) to address the continued technological expansion of document production and reproduction. Attending to the social and technological specificity of document production challenges the transhistorical logic with which the discourse of print culture approaches materially distinct media phenomena. In addition, "print culture" then serves as a foil for those who claim a radical break with modernity, defined by the dominance of "print," in the name of the digital. "Better instead to resist," Gitelman argues, "any but local and contrastive logics for media; better to look for meanings that arise, shift, and persist according to the uses that media—emergent, dominant, residual—familiarly have" (9). The "know-show function" of documents demands that we see the trees in the forest rather than lose them in the canopy of print culture or new media and submit to their techno-determinist frameworks.

Responding to the provocations of the introduction, the book's four chapters and afterword attempt to mobilize the "know-show function" through specific case studies of document production. Arranged chronologically, these chapters examine, respectively, nineteenth-century job printing, typescript, Xerox, and *.pdf, without attempting to give an account of the transition from one media to another. Instead, each chapter presents a particular historical episode in the production of documents in an attempt to specify the ways each medium produces a particular variation on the overall logic of the genre (the document). This logic, what the documents "know-show," is the social primacy of bureaucracy and the institutional forms of modern capitalism (including universities and governmental agencies). The document embodies the anonymity of its producers and the instrumentality of its uses; job printing of "blanks"—forms, ledgers, notebooks, and so on—is implicitly offered as a paradigmatic form since blanks have neither authors nor readers but exist only to be "filled out" and filed. Of course, the central example Gitelman turns to is not, in fact, a blank but *Harpel's Typograph Or Book of Specimens, Containing Useful Information and a Collection of Examples of Letterpress Job Printing, Arranged for the Assistance of Master Printers, Amateurs, Apprentices, and Others*. As this lengthy and exhaustive title already suggests (know-shows), this "document" belongs not to the bureaucratic corporation but the art and trade of printing. Gitelman acknowledges the changing landscape of printing and organized labor in the late nineteenth century but focuses on certain job printers' self-conception of their trade in formal terms. In this sense, Harpel's book is anything but exemplary (and it is unclear how influential it was), evincing instead the articulation of a professional aesthetic standard for job printing. While this certainly eschews the synoptic reduction of blanks, for example, to the letterpress, it says little about the specificity of blanks of any sort, which remain anonymous generalities. Ripe as the quotidian job printed documents are for excavating the constitution, workings, and power of large-scale state and corporate institutions, Harpel's text and the chapter's other primary examples say little about the changing organizational forms of capitalist modernity or their use of documents. Dwelling instead on collections of "specimens" rather than any specimens themselves, as though this yields a clear sense of the document's role in this moment in social and media history, this initial case study appears more interested in these odd, perhaps neglected, trade publications as reflections of a certain subjectivity than in explicating the importance of blanks as documents of either this history or a particular media technology.

Whether the blank, the typescript book, the photocopy, or the *.pdf file, *Paper Knowledge* follows this pattern of focusing on atypical cases of document production and reproduction—largely commentaries on methods of reproduction—which are noteworthy for being neither quotidian nor anonymous yet are offered as indicative of the far-reaching social characteristics of documents produced by particular media technologies. This approach is most effective in the two middle chapters, devoted to typescript and photocopying, where their "know-show" function clearly, if implicitly, addresses the changing place of documents in twentieth-century American institutions and culture even as little is done to elucidate this connection.

Repeating the gesture of the job printing case, the typescript chapter details the emergence of practices and standards that now constitute the core of academic work through Robert C. Binkley's *Methods of Reproducing Research Materials*. Commissioned in 1930 by the American Council of Learned Societies and the Social Science Research Council's "Joint Committee on Materials for Research" and published by the company that would spawn University Microfilms International and eventually ProQuest, Gitelman positions Binkley's response to the interwar problem of reproducing research as encapsulating a previous historical conjuncture—when the university and its scholars were solidly situated as mediators between the state, the public, and private enterprise—while foreshadowing the contemporary academy and its neoliberal reconfiguration. Thus Binkley's report is a Janus-faced document, at once advocating for expanded access to and dissemination of research materials and scholarly work made possible by reproductive media while also acting as an accessory to the rise of the "scholarly monograph" as the gold standard for tenure and the attendant changes in academic labor (59). On the other hand, Gitelman, in the succeeding chapter, details Daniel Ellsberg's xeroxing of the confidential Department of Defense dossier on the history of U.S. intervention in Vietnam (i.e., the Pentagon Papers) as an instantiation of the nexus between institutional document reproduction and personal copying created by photocopying. If the ostensibly standards-driven texts of the previous chapters acted as evidence of emergent self-consciousness around particular institutions and technologies of document production and reproduction, Ellsberg's versioning of the stolen dossier represent the almost compulsive duplication, manipulation, and dissemination of documents that the Xerox introduced. As Gitelman writes, "Xerographic reproduction offered a way to edit or remake the 'History of U.S. Decision Making Process on Vietnam Policy' as well as to expropriate it," which, at the same time, became a form of self-making enabled by "xerography" as a mode of making, publishing, and archiving by and for the general public through the spread of copy shops, especially around universities, and office work (89). In both these cases the central "documents" are much more clearly implicated in the changing status of documents in the ever-more intense routinization of life under "managerial capital" and the proliferating uses for media technologies.

All of this said, even these chapters of *Paper Knowledge* are nagged by problems around what the relation is between evidence and argument when it comes to documents, as well as media technology. The detailed, often narrative expositions of case studies, blending short historical descriptions with specific analytic claims, may counter the homogenizing aspect of "print culture" but at the cost of directly engaging the broader social field and political stakes surrounding documents and their uses. For instance, despite the repeated invocation of "managerial capital," little sustained attention is given to historical shifts in labor either in specific industries, such as printing, or more generally. Nor is the dynamic of private and public technology development and use, exemplified in Ellsberg's theft of the Pentagon Papers from the RAND Corporation and central to the rise of neoliberal governance and economics, explored beyond cursory mentions. Perhaps pursuing these strands ventures further toward the speculative aspect of this media history than *Paper Knowledge* aims for, but the historical data these episodes dole out does not quite amount to a history either. Indeed, the fascination with a certain empirical materiality—these trade publications exist, have these characteristics, and were produced this way—appears to draw Gitelman, and perhaps the entire turn toward documents, in the direction of an uncanny positivism. Caught between the dread poles of theoretical excess and an overt embrace of the self-evident function of documents for historical research, the force of argument—that is, that which animates the document as it traverses new historical encounters—is sacrificed in the name of "local and contrastive logics for media."

In this sense, the book is undercut by its own impetus. With the "know-show function," Gitelman foregrounds paper documents as enigmatic objects whose evidentiary value is only ever actualized through their use as "clues" but never quite articulates what they are clues to. Thus, the book's deployment of documents and careful detailing of their production and reproduction ironically treats them as though they simply "know-show" the book's argument through description and documentation, transparently rendering the social, historical, and political stakes that presumably motivate the text. As a reader I am very sympathetic to the text's effort to affirm the material specificity of documents and its complicating effect on evidentiary discourse, but *Paper Knowledge*, to return to the cliché, risks losing the forest for the trees in its effort to attend to the specifics of (certain) entries in the media genre of documents. Perhaps rather than attempting to enumerate each species of document within the woods of media history, it would be better to treat documents as bread crumbs offering multiple paths through the forest, whose directions and destinations are contingent on what it is we ask of them as well as what responses they make possible.

Benedict Stork is adjunct instructor in Seattle University's film studies program. He works at the intersection of documentary, critical theory, and politics. He has published on documentary and the concept of history, as well as on politics and aesthetics in online videos of police violence.

NEW MAPS FOR THE DIASPORA

ESCAPE FROM NEW YORK: THE NEW NEGRO RENAISSANCE BEYOND HARLEM
EDITED BY DAVARIAN L. BALDWIN AND MINKAH MAKALANI
University of Minnesota Press, 2013

Arlene R. Keizer

In her recent book *Physics of Blackness,* Michelle Wright argues that blackness is not a what—it's always a when and a where. While Wright uses this formulation to analyze the present and future of the African Diaspora, readers delving into *Escape from New York: The New Negro Renaissance beyond Harlem* will recognize that the anthology has been conceived and organized according to the same principle. Though many scholars have noted that the new consciousness developing within people of African descent in the first third of the twentieth century was by no means confined to Harlem, this collection of essays registers the polyvalent, internationalist, and coalition-building character of the New Negro movement more comprehensively than any other text to date.

Escape from New York is essential reading for those who study and teach black modernism, black internationalism, and the Harlem Renaissance, as well as the African, Caribbean, and European movements with which the Harlem Renaissance is associated. Historians, literary critics, and researchers examining culture, politics, and social movements will find here essays that help to reshape notions of black agency, both individual and collective, across this wide sphere of action. Yet as satisfying as this volume is in its main task of situating the New Negro in a broader politico-geographic frame, its main editor Davarian Baldwin acknowledges in his introduction that it "constitutes *a field in formation*" (4, emphasis in original) rather than inserting the last pieces into the puzzle of black life between World War I and World War II. While immeasurably enhancing the existing work on the New Negro, this book also offers multiple points of entry for new scholarship.

In addition to Baldwin's fine introduction, many other essays in *Escape from New York* are worthy of special notice. In his cogent foreword to the collection, Robin D. G. Kelley asks, "Why revisit the New Negro now?" He argues persuasively that the persistent power of "settler colonialism and racial capitalism" and the need for "multiracial coalitions" to "bring an end to these forms of domination" makes this volume a critical resource for the present and future domestic and international struggles of undocumented immigrants, stateless individuals and communities, and citizens fighting against "the privatization of schools, hospitals, public transit, public housing, and the dismantling of public-sector unions" (x–xi). The genealogies linking the New Negro to early twenty-first-century battles are especially clear in Shannon King's "Not Just a World Problem: Segregation, Police Brutality, and New Negro Politics in New York City" and Anastasia Curwood's "New Negro Marriages and the Everyday Challenges of Upward Mobility," which reveal how forms of striving toward racial and gender equality and citizenship by black men and women resulted in significant, positive changes. But these and other essays also register the profound toll such striving took on black subjects invested in living up to New Negro ideals. King's historical work is critical for the present moment, in which long histories of black subjugation under police oppression in places like Ferguson, Missouri, are finally coming to light. Curwood's essay offers a crucial corrective to hysterical current arguments about the failure of marriage as an institution for African Americans, in which a sense of black cultural deficiency underlies even the most well-meaning analyses. Curwood narrates and critiques the way that profound desires to establish and maintain marriages in which male breadwinners supported female housewives destroyed some black individuals and relationships when economic realities made such marriages impossible.

Given this collection's title, it will come as no surprise that some of the most notable contributions are those situating the New Negro movement in new or refurbished international frameworks. David Luis-Brown, in his intriguing "Cuban *Negrismo,* Mexican *Indigenismo*: Contesting Neocolonialism in the New Negro Movement," employs "alternative primitivism" as a "distinctly transnational tool that could be used in critiques of U.S. neocolonialism" rather than as a form of Euro-American nostalgia and racial denigration (54–55). Minkah

Makalani, coeditor of the anthology, revisits C. L. R. James's early years in London in his essay "An International African Opinion: Amy Ashwood Garvey and C. L. R. James in Black Radical London." Tracing the evolution of James's thought through his political involvement with Amy Ashwood Garvey and George Padmore in the 1930s, Makalani shows how Garvey in particular helped James to move beyond his view of Africa as backward. As Makalani's essay encourages us to see London anew as a site of black radical organizing, Jennifer Wilks trains a fresh lens on Paris in "Black Modernist Women at the Parisian Crossroads." Analyzing female figures in the works of the Martinican intellectual Paulette Nardal and the African American novelist Jessie Fauset, Wilks treats the City of Light "as an instrumental modernist crossroads where, through geographic and cultural dislocation, black women writers . . . negotiated intersecting categories of identity in their own lives as well as in those of their characters" (228). This essay recognizes the very particular viewpoints of educated black women travelers from the Americas and utilizes those viewpoints to render our understanding of the metropole even more complex.

One of the most impressive aspects of *Escape from New York* as a scholarly volume is its investment in the conceptual work of limning the New Negro movement. Baldwin's introduction "announces the New Negro as an analytic" (4), and Michelle Ann Stephens's article "The Conjunctural Field of New Negro Studies" critically reinterprets a widespread understanding of the New Negro as a "a rhetorical figure" or "a purely aesthetic category" (401–2). Of course, it is Henry Louis Gates Jr.'s influential essay "The Trope of a New Negro and the Reconstruction of the Image of the Black" that established this interpretation of the Harlem Renaissance. In response, many of the authors collected here find it important to emphasize the forgotten lived experiences of "New Negroes." Stephens' piece, which should really appear last because of the way that it responds to the introduction and the volume as a whole, offers a stunning theoretical analysis of the book. She writes,

> What seems to me to be the most important point behind this collection's emphasis on black historical experience is the paradigm-shifting observation about the deeper hegemonic crisis that the study of the New Negro reveals, as a conjunctural epiphenomenon articulated to the literary, the artistic, the cultural, the social, the private, the psychological, the

economic, the military, and the political simultaneously, in an ensemble of geo-historical relations that come to a head at the turn and in the early decades of the twentieth century. (404)

Stephens goes on to situate all the essays in the volume within the contexts of the consolidations and crises of empire, colonial modernity, and patriarchal gender relations, identifying these as the period's most significant conjunctural vectors. Few anthologies meditate upon their own construction as carefully as *Escape from New York* does.

My final note to the reader is *buy this book!* Don't wait your turn to check it out of the library.

Arlene R. Keizer is associate professor of English, comparative literature, and African American studies at the University of California, Irvine. Her essays have appeared in *African American Review, American Literary History, PMLA,* and other journals. A first-generation American born to Trinidadian parents, she visits the ocean almost every day.

BOOKS RECEIVED

Adamson, Joni, William A. Gleason, and David N. Pellow, eds. *Keywords for Environmental Studies*. New York: New York University Press, 2016.

Alvarez, Steven J. *Selling War: A Critical Look at the Military's PR Machine*. Lincoln, Neb.: Potomac Books, 2016.

Apap, Christopher C. *The Genius of Place: The Geographic Imagination in the Early Republic*. Lebanon: University of New Hampshire Press, 2016.

Badiou, Alain, and Nicolas Truong. *In Praise of Theatre*. Malden, Mass.: Polity Press, 2015.

Bérubé, Michael. *The Secret Life of Stories: From Don Quixote to Harry Potter, How Understanding Intellectual Disability Transforms the Way We Read*. New York: New York University Press, 2016.

Blocker, Jane. *Becoming Past: History in Contemporary Art*. Minneapolis: University of Minnesota Press, 2016.

Brienza, Casey. *Manga in America: Translational Book Publishing and the Domestication of Japanese Comics*. New York: Bloomsbury, 2016.

Broinowski, Adam. *Cultural Responses to Occupation in Japan: The Performing Body during and after the Cold War*. New York: Bloomsbury, 2016.

Brøvig-Hanssen, Ragnhild, and Anne Danielsen. *Digital Signatures: The Impact of Digitization on Popular Music Sound*. Cambridge, Mass.: MIT Press, 2016.

Cahan, Susan E. *Mounting Frustration: The Art Museum in the Age of Black Power*. Durham: Duke University Press, 2016.

Cai, Xiang. *Revolution and Its Narratives: China's Socialist Literary and Cultural Imaginaries, 1949–1966*. Trans. and ed. Rebecca E. Karl and Xueping Zhong. Durham: Duke University Press, 2016.

Carrington, André. *Speculative Blackness: The Future of Race in Science Fiction*. Minneapolis: University of Minnesota Press, 2016.

Casper, Monica J., and Eric Wertheimer. *Critical Trauma Studies: Understanding Violence, Conflict, and Memory in Everyday Life*. New York: New York University Press, 2016.

Cheah, Pheng. *What Is a World? On Postcolonial Literature as World Literature*. Durham: Duke University Press, 2016.

Chion, Michel. *Sound: An Acoulogical Treatise*. Trans. James A. Steintrager. Durham: Duke University Press, 2016.

Cohen, Jeffrey Jerome, and Lowell Duckert, eds. *Elemental Ecocriticism: Thinking with Earth, Air, Water, and Fire*. Minneapolis: University of Minnesota Press, 2015.

Coles, Romand. *Visionary Pragmatism: Radical and Ecological Democracy in Neoliberal Times*. Durham: Duke University Press, 2016.

Collier, Delinda. *Repainting the Walls of Lunda: Information Colonialism and Angolan Art*. Minneapolis: University of Minnesota Press, 2016.

Crosby, Christina. *A Body, Undone: Living on after Great Pain*. New York: New York University Press, 2016.

Derrida, Jacques. *Of Grammatology*. Trans. Gayatri Charkravorty Spivak. Introduction by Judith Butler. Baltimore: Johns Hopkins University Press, 2016.

Eidsheim, Nina Sun. *Sensing Sound: Singing and Listening as Vibrational Practice*. Durham: Duke University Press, 2015.

Ellcessor, Elizabeth. *Restricted Access: Media, Disability, and the Politics of Participation*. New York: New York University Press, 2016.

Galli, Carlo. *Janus's Gaze: Essays on Carl Schmitt*. Ed. Adam Sitze. Trans. Amanda Minervini. Durham: Duke University Press, 2015.

George, Sheldon. *Trauma and Race: A Lacanian Study of African American Racial Identity*. Waco, Tex.: Baylor University Press, 2016.

Glick, Jeremy Matthew. *The Black Radical Tragic: Performance, Aesthetics, and the Unfinished Haitian Revolution*. New York: New York University Press, 2016.

Gray, Mary L., Colin R. Johnson, and Brian J. Gilley, eds. *Queering the Countryside: New Frontiers in Rural Queer Studies*. New York: New York University Press, 2016.

Grüttemeier, Ralf. *Literary Trials: Exceptio Artis and Theories of Literature in Court*. New York: Bloomsbury, 2016.

Hanna, Monica, Jennifer Harford Vargas, and José David Saldívar, eds. *Junot Díaz and the Decolonial Imagination*. Durham: Duke University Press, 2016.

Herkenhoff, Ferreira. *Mário Pedrosa: Primary Documents*. New York: The Museum of Modern Art, 2015.

Hodgkinson, Tim. *Music and the Myth of Wholeness: Toward a New Aesthetic Paradigm*. Cambridge, Mass.: MIT Press, 2016.

Honeywill, Ross. *The Man Problem: Destructive Masculinity in Western Culture*. London: Palgrave Macmillan, 2016.

Hunt, Nancy Rose. *A Nervous State: Violence, Remedies, and Reverie in Colonial Congo*. Durham: Duke University Press, 2016.

Kauffman, Stuart A. *Humanity in a Creative Universe*. London: Oxford University Press, 2016.

King, Richard C. *Redskins: Insult and Brand*. Lincoln: University of Nebraska Press, 2016.

LaRocca, David, and Ricardo Miguel-Alfonso, eds. *A Power to Translate the World: New Essays on Emerson and International Culture*. Lebanon: Dartmouth College Press, 2015.

Laruelle, François. *General Theory of Victims*. Trans. Jessie Hock and Alex Dubilet. Malden, Mass.: Polity Press, 2015.

Lempert, Lora Bex. *Women Doing Life: Gender, Punishment, and the Struggle for Identity*. New York: New York University Press, 2016.

Lunning, Frenchy, ed. *Mechademia. Vol. 10, World Renewal*. Minneapolis: University of Minnesota Press, 2015.

McHugh, Roland. *Annotations to Finnegans Wake*. 4th ed. Baltimore: Johns Hopkins University Press, 2016.

Meisel, Martin. *Chaos Imagined: Literature, Art, Science*. New York: Columbia University Press, 2016.

Mendoza, Victor Román. *Metroimperial Intimacies: Fantasy, Racial-Sexual Governance, and the Philippines in U.S. Imperialism, 1899–1913*. Durham: Duke University Press, 2015.

Mose, Tamara R. *The Playdate: Parents, Children, and the New Expectations of Play*. New York: New York University Press, 2016.

Negri, Antonio. *Pipeline: Letters from Prison*. Trans. Ed Emery. Malden, Mass.: Polity Press, 2014.

Panzer, Joe. *The Process That Is the World: Cage/Deleuze/Events/Performance*. New York: Bloomsbury, 2016.

Payne, Matthew. *Playing War: Military Video Games after 9/11*. New York: New York University Press, 2016.

Penix-Tadsen, Phillip. *Cultural Code: Video Games and Latin America*. Cambridge, Mass.: MIT Press, 2016.

Picouly, Daniel. *The Leopard Boy: A Novel*. Trans. Jeanne Garane. Charlottesville: The University of Virginia Press, 2016.

Pierce, Steven. *Moral Economies of Corruption: State Formation and Political Culture in Nigeria*. Durham: Duke University Press, 2016.

Radano, Ronald, and Tejumola Olaniyan, eds. *Audible Empire: Music, Global Politics, Critique*. Durham: Duke University Press, 2016.

Rawlinson, Mary C. *Just Life: Bioethics and the Future of Sexual Difference*. New York: Columbia University Press, 2016.

Roberts, Brian Russel, and Keith Foulcher, eds. *Indonesian Notebook: A Sourcebook on Richard Wright and the Bandung Conference*. Durham: Duke University Press, 2016.

Rothman, Barbara Katz. *A Bun in the Oven: How the Food and Birth Movements Resist Industrialization*. New York: New York University Press, 2016.

Ruda, Frank. *Abolishing Freedom: A Plea for a Contemporary Use of Fatalism*. Lincoln: University of Nebraska Press, 2016.

Salvato, Nick. *Obstruction*. Durham: Duke University Press, 2016.

Schmitt, Carl. *Dialogues on Power and Space*. Ed. Andreas Kalyvas and Federico Finchelstein. Trans. Samuel Garrett Zeitilin. Malden, Mass.: Polity Press, 2015.

Schock, Kurt. *Civil Resistance Today*. Malden, Mass.: Polity Press, 2015.

Schuster, Aaron. *The Trouble with Pleasure: Deleuze and Psychoanalysis*. Cambridge, Mass.: MIT Press, 2016.

Schwartz, Margaret. *Dead Matter: The Meaning of Iconic Corpses.* Minneapolis: University of Minnesota Press, 2015.

Seltzer, Mark. *The Official World.* Durham: Duke University Press, 2016.

Shu, Yuan, and Donald E. Pease, eds. *American Studies as Transnational Practice: Turning toward the Transpacific.* Lebanon: Dartmouth College Press, 2015.

Skaria, Ajay. *Unconditional Equality: Gandhi's Religion of Resistance.* Minneapolis: University of Minnesota Press, 2016.

Tee, Charles T. *Ingenious Citizenship: Recreating Democracy for Social Change.* Durham: Duke University Press, 2016.

Thangaraj, Stanley I., Constancio R. Arnaldo, Jr., and Christina B. Chin, eds. *Asian American Sporting Cultures.* New York: New York University Press, 2016.

Toal, Catherine. *The Entrapments of Form: Cruelty and Modern Literature.* New York: Fordham University Press, 2016.

Wilmer, S. E., and Audrone Zukauskaite, eds. *Resisting Biopolitics: Philosophical, Political, and Performative Strategies.* New York: Routledge, 2016.

Woldoff, Rachael A., Lisa M. Morrison, and Michael R. Glass. *Priced Out: Stuyvesant Town and the Loss of Middle-Class Neighborhoods.* New York: New York University Press, 2016.

FROM THE
NORTH AMERICAN
REVIEW PRESS

CALL FOR SUBMISSIONS

•Excerpts up to 50 pages
from an unpublished literary
crime novel

•Selected by Grant Tracey
for publication by the **North
American Review Press**

•Visit our website:
northamericanreview.org for
more information

NEW TITLES

 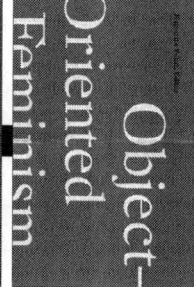  

Inter/Nationalism
Decolonizing Native America and Palestine
Steven Salaita

$22.95 | $80.50 cloth | 232 pages
Indigenous Americas Series
Available November 2016

Object-Oriented Feminism
Katherine Behar, editor

$27.00 paper | $94.50 cloth | 296 pages
Available November 2016

Foucault in Iran
Islamic Revolution after the Enlightenment
Behrooz Ghamari-Tabrizi

$27.00 paper | $94.50 cloth | 272 pages
Muslim International Series

Indirect Action
Schizophrenia, Epilepsy, AIDS, and the Course of Health Activism
Lisa Diedrich

$28.00 paper | $98.00 cloth | 312 pages
Available December 2016

Human Programming
Brainwashing, Automatons, and American Unfreedom
Scott Selisker

$26.00 paper | $91.00 cloth | 272 pages

Exposed
Environmental Politics and Pleasures in Posthuman Times
Stacy Alaimo

$27.00 paper | $94.50 cloth | 256 pages
Available October 2016

A Curriculum of Fear
Homeland Security in U.S. Public Schools
Nicole Nguyen

$26.00 paper | $91.00 cloth | 296 pages

Holidays in the Danger Zone
Entanglements of War and Tourism
Debbie Lisle

$30.00 paper | $105.00 cloth | 408 pages
Critical War Studies Series

Beautiful Wasteland
The Rise of Detroit as America's Postindustrial Frontier
Rebecca J. Kinney

$25.00 paper | $87.50 cloth | 248 pages
Available November 2016

For the Children?
Protecting Innocence in a Carceral State
Erica R. Meiners

$27.00 paper | $94.50 cloth | 264 pages
Available October 2016

FROM MINNESOTA

 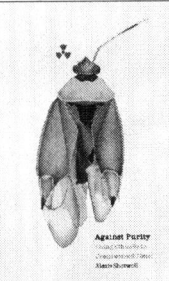  

The Servant Class City
Urban Revitalization versus the Working Poor in San Diego
David J. Karjanen

$28.00 paper | $98.00 cloth | 312 pages
Globalization and Community Series, vol. 25

Against Purity
Living Ethically in Compromised Times
Alexis Shotwell

$27.00 paper | $94.50 cloth | 256 pages
Available December 2016

Predator Empire
Drone Warfare and Full Spectrum Dominance
Ian G. R. Shaw

$28.00 paper | $98.00 cloth | 336 pages

Anti-Book
On the Art and Politics of Radical Publishing
Nicholas Thoburn

$30.00 paper | $105.00 cloth | 368 pages
Cultural Critique Books Series
Available December 2016

Living Cargo
How Black Britain Performs Its Past
Steven Blevins

$30.00 paper | $105.00 cloth | 360 pages
Available October 2016

Downed by Friendly Fire
Black Girls, White Girls, and Suburban Schooling
Signithia Fordham

$25.00 paper | $87.50 cloth | 320 pages
Available November 2016

Urban Policy in the Time of Obama
James DeFilippis, editor
Afterword by Cedric Johnson

$30.00 paper | $105.00 cloth | 368 pages
Globalization and Community Series, vol. 26
Available November 2016

Testing Fate
Tay-Sachs Disease and the Right to Be Responsible
Shelley Z. Reuter

$27.00 paper | $84.50 cloth | 280 pages

Brown Threat
Identification in the Security State
Kumarini Silva

$27.00 paper | $94.50 cloth | 240 pages
Available November 2016

First Strike
Educational Enclosures in Black Los Angeles
Damien M. Sojoyner

$27.00 paper | $94.50 cloth | 288 pages
Available October 2016

University of Minnesota Press • 800-621-2736 • www.upress.umn.edu